LinkAges

Planning an Intergenerational Program for Preschool

MERLE D. GRIFF
DONNA LAMBERT
DOROTHY FRUIT
MARY DELLMAN-JENKINS

Innovative Learning Publications

Addison-Wesley Publishing Company
Menlo Park, California • Reading, Massachusetts • New York
Don Mills, Ontario • Wokingham, England • Amsterdam • Bonn
Paris • Milan • Madrid • Sydney • Singapore • Tokyo • Seoul
Taipei • Mexico City • San Juan

This book is published by Innovative Learning Publications™, an imprint of the Alternative Publishing Group of Addison-Wesley Publishing Company.

Senior Editor:	Lois Fowkes
Design Manager:	Jeff Kelly
Production Manager:	Janet Yearian
Production Coordinator:	Barbara Atmore
Cover and text design:	London Road Design
Cover illustration:	Margaret Sanfilippo
Illustrations:	Margaret Sanfilippo and Rachel Gage

ISBN 0-201-49427-2

1 2 3 4 5 6 7 8 9 10-ML-99-98 97 96 95

ACKNOWLEDGMENTS

Our appreciation goes to Jody Strickling and Tammie Reed for allowing us to include some of the intergenerational activities that they have developed; Laura Foster for assisting us as a "field reader" and for sharing her professional intergenerational experiences; Stacy Smith and Patricia Noel for always being willing to type yet another set of corrections and changes; and to all the practicum students who worked with us during the research phase of this project.

Special thanks to the following people for their diligent writing in the following sections:
Activity Analysis - Karen VanderVen, Ph.D.
Curriculum Web - Catherine Blount, M.A.
Critical Review - Holly Borden

Contributing Editors

Rebecca Foster
Deborah DelCorso

Our most sincere thanks to all the older adults, the children, and their families, who have brought joy and understanding into all of our lives.

FUNDED BY THE ROBERTA CHAMBERLIN FOUNDATION

CONTENTS

Section 1:
PLANNING THE PROGRAM

INTERGENERATIONAL PROGRAMMING: A BRIEF HISTORY

The attitudes and behaviors children have about old age can have important implications for intergenerational relationships; in our aging society we need to make strengthening these relationships a priority. Evidence is growing that regular interactions between young children and older adults have a positive effect both on the development and learning of young children and on older persons' quality of life (Lyons, 1986). One way to strengthen their relationship is to bring these two age groups together through intergenerational programs. These programs are designed to provide environments in which preschool children and older adults will feel accepted and important in a culture that is reluctant to recognize their worth.

The concept of intergenerational programming was pioneered in 1963 with the Foster Grandparent Program. It continued as a major area of emphasis in the 1969 development of the Retired Senior Volunteer Program (RSVP) and the (1969) National Center for Service-Learning. Advocacy efforts begun in 1970 by the Gray Panthers resulted in an ongoing interest in intergenerational programs at the regional and national levels. Subsequently, in 1975, the Administration on Aging encouraged members of aging and education networks to develop a service plan for older adults to carry out in schools.

As the number of intergenerational programs continued to increase, the National Council on Aging, in cooperation with the Child Welfare League of America, created the first intergenerational network. In 1980 their efforts resulted in a consortium of national senior and youth agencies that recognize the interdependence of youth and adults, known as Generations United.

Why We Need to Bring the Generations Together

It is a fact of life, call it human nature, that we tend to fear that which we do not understand. Along with this lack of understanding is the tendency to ignore these fears and hope that they will go away. One example of this unwillingness and/or fear to understand the "strange" or "unfamiliar" is the attitude expressed toward the elderly in our society and toward the process of aging.

In a society obsessed with youth, in a culture in which old age and elders have often been ignored rather than revered for their life experiences, this fear and lack of tolerance has perpetuated itself. The same may also be said of conceptions and misconceptions regarding the handicapped or the developmentally disabled. How often have we noticed another person, or possibly ourselves, staring at a blind person walking down the street or at an elder who may be speaking too loudly in a public place? This is simply human nature—curiosity about things we don't understand. Those with frailties or disabilities seem outside the realm of our daily lives and our understanding.

Only in the past ten to fifteen years have attitudes toward the elderly, the handicapped, and the developmentally disabled begun to change. In this book, our primary focus will be on the elderly—specifically, major refinements that have occurred in eldercare and in health care for the elderly.

Two significant factors have caused a tremendous growth in programs available to elders and improvements in facilities to care for them: (1) Dedicated, caring professionals have continued to voice their concern for meeting the needs of a rapidly increasing number of older adults; and (2) Society finally realized that prolonged lifespans go hand-in-hand with the added responsibility of caring for an ever-increasing population of the elderly. We who are younger are aware that we will require the same care and concern as we age.

As a result of this increased acceptance of aging, ideas have become realities. Some of the resulting programs include:

- Continuum of care facilities, which offer a spectrum of services for elders—independent living, assisted living, and intermediate and skilled nursing care;
- Adult day care for the elderly, which provides supervised care for older adults who return to their families in the evening; and
- Elder hostel (continuing education based on college campuses) and other such programs, which offer opportunities for active and independent elders.

HOW DO INTERGENERATIONAL PROGRAMS WORK?

Intergenerational programs encompass older adults, usually over the age of sixty, and children from infancy through adolescence. In this book, we will focus on programs that include elders and preschoolers. The primary goal of intergenerational programs is to encourage a positive attitude among children toward older adults and the aging process in general.

At the heart of intergenerational programs is the idea that they should be mutually beneficial to members of both generations because they foster growth, understanding, and friendship between the old and the young (Newman, 1986). Intergenerational programs usually meet on a regular basis. Having a group of children visit with older adults in a nursing home only once a year for a holiday program is simply not enough contact for the children and elders to form meaningful relationships or to promote understanding between the generations.

Establishing a Program—The Ups and Downs That Lead To Success

Although the idea that bringing children and their elders together might be beneficial for both generations is easy to support, some pitfalls and stumbling blocks are inevitable in the process. Even with positive input, few programs have ever reached completion with a totally positive, problem-free outcome. Programmatic development is often more a matter of two steps forward and one step backward. This handbook is designed to alert you to these possible problems and to provide guidelines needed to make your program one that benefits everyone.

Success is the bottom line! Any program flourishes through trial and error, by recognizing the problems and finding workable solutions. Despite the abundance of new programs, facilities, and options for older adults that have developed seemingly overnight, the positive change in attitude has taken many decades. Through hard work and persistence, an idea whose time has come—intergenerational programs—has now become a successful reality.

BENEFITS FOR PRESCHOOL CHILDREN

Children today are often unable to see extended family members frequently, for many reasons. These include the increased mobility of family members, an increasing divorce rate, the breakdown of the extended family, and other current societal issues. Because contact between generations no longer occurs naturally, it must now be "consciously orchestrated" (Waters, 1991). The benefits of intergenerational programs for children, however, outweigh the extra effort needed to make them work. These benefits include:

Caring: The director of a child daycare program commented, "Our intergenerational program gave our children a knowledge of and respect for the elders. The children also learned of the past in a unique way. But, more importantly, they learned to care. Helping the children to nurture the elders as well as to be nurtured themselves—to care about someone else—is essential to us as teachers." (Foster, 1993).

Tolerance and understanding: Many preschool teachers view intergenerational programs as part of their anti-bias curriculum. Fear and uncertainty of older adults is often expressed by both children and staff members. These prejudices form the bases for the decision to include intergenerational programs in their curriculums.

Self-esteem: Older adults often have the time to direct all of their attention to the children's thoughts and ideas in ways that are supportive and loving. A staff member from the McKinley Centre Intergenerational Project was reminded of this recently when she saw Cara, a graduate of the program, who had just entered first grade in a local elementary school and was attending the extended day program at her new school. Noticing tears running down Cara's cheeks, the staff member approached her to offer some comfort, when Cara suddenly raised her head and whispered, "It's awfully lonely in this new school—there aren't any grandmas or grandpas here to hold you when you're scared."

Knowledge: Intergenerational programs help perpetuate cultures and value systems that might otherwise be lost. Older adults relate fascinating stories about growing up, games and sports that they used to play, holidays and other special events, famous people that they knew, and even how daily routines such as preparing meals and washing clothes were done in the past.

As an example, one of our older adults brought in a washboard. She explained how the washboard had been used, and demonstrated the proper technique for getting clothes clean. The children used it to wash rags and towels in the water table, enjoying this activity for a long period of time.

Another older adult told a group of wide-eyed children about milking a cow and soaking cheesecloths in the milk. The cheesecloths were then hung on a clothesline to sour and the drippings were made into cottage cheese. "Can you imagine cheese from a clothesline?" asked the older adult. "By the way, what is clothesline?" asked one little boy.

Behavior management: Interactions with older adults can be used to assist children during difficult periods of the day such as naptime and waiting to be picked up at the end of the day. Elders are often helpful in providing children with special attention they may require during these frequently difficult transitional times. Staff members also appreciate this support.

Individual attention: Children want and need individualized attention. Grandmas and grandpas have the time to devote their full attention to just one child. In our childcare center, for example, there are infants who need almost constant rocking and attention. One infant, Adrianna, wanted to be held for most of the day. By having a "grandma" available for a few extra hours every day, Adrianna was extremely content. This grandma felt important as a warm and loving presence as well.

BENEFITS FOR OLDER ADULTS

Elders are affected by many of the same factors that impact children. Older adults can suffer from a feeling of isolation and a lack of caring. They may often experience feelings of loneliness, frustration, and uselessness. These feelings can be eased, however, when elders are actively involved in an intergenerational program.

Some benefits of intergenerational programs for older adults are:

Increased self-esteem: "It is important to an older person's sense of self-esteem to be acknowledged by the young as an elder, to have one's life experience seen as interesting and valuable" (Reville, 1989, p. 50).

Reduced isolation: Older adults strongly need to believe that they are still an important part of their society; to feel useful and important, not "thrown away" without the opportunity to impart their wisdom and heritage.

Sense of purpose: The following quotes are taken from the writings of older adults following their participation in an intergenerational arts program. They say it better than we ever could.

> "What I respected most was the way she listened to me. She made me feel my words had worth." (Goodman, 1993, p. 31).

> "Recently widowed, trying to adjust without my best friend and life's companion, I did not seem to be able to call upon any of the activities that had filled my life before. That has changed now. I suddenly feel creative and am bursting with ideas. . . . I no longer hesitate to buy green bananas." (Speert, 1993, p. 57).

Additional program benefits for children and elders may be found in Table 1, page 95.

Intergenerational programs can also benefit the staff members who participate. The Executive Director of the McKinley Centre Early Childhood Program commented to us:

> "One day some of the children and I were delivering flowers in the nursing home. We passed by the room of a man who was mumbling and drooling. I found his behavior so unsettling that I did not plan to enter his room. Suddenly Delno, one of our three-year-olds, walked up to the side of his bed, patted his arm and said, 'Hey, there's somebody here. Open your eyes. We've brung you some flowers and I'm just goin' give you a little hug here.' The man stopped mumbling, looked at Delno, and slowly smiled. I realized that I had been unable to reach out to this man, but a three-year-old was able to look past things that I could not, creating a beautiful and warm moment between himself and this elder.

> "I've never forgotten what this experience taught me. I do reach out now and touch. For example, if I am in the grocery store and an older person stops to tell me a story or ask a question, I will listen now—I realize that these few moments of my time are important to the elder. I, too, have become a different person through our intergenerational program. It has brought a new dimension of caring into my life." (Foster, 1993)

CHOOSING A SETTING FOR INTERGENERATIONAL EXPERIENCES

There are a variety of ways in which intergenerational experiences can be provided. The following are some examples:

Planned contact at the children's setting with older adults, or planned contact in such older adult settings as senior centers, adult daycare centers, or nursing homes. The older adults may be community elders, representatives from senior groups such as the American Association of Retired Persons, the local Y.W.C.A./Y.M.C.A., or participants in the programs listed above.

In this setting, the children and the elders meet on a weekly or biweekly schedule and participate in activities planned by both teachers and eldercare staff. The distinctive characteristic of these groups is equal and joint participation. *LinkAges* is designed to address this type of intergenerational program, although many of the principles discussed apply to other kinds of intergenerational experiences.

Regular contact in the child setting with individual elder volunteers who participate according to a prearranged schedule. These are usually community elders who require a flexible schedule. Community elders are willing to make a commitment for limited periods of time. This may be for two hours a week or just for certain times of the year, such as only in the fall and the spring. Community elders are usually a tremendous asset for any child center, but they must be cautioned about notifying your center of changes or modifications in their schedules, in advance, when possible. How much advance time is required will differ according to each center's needs. Regular contact may also include older adults who wish to host a special "class" on a weekly or monthly basis. Activity groups that have been successful include a music class taught by a retired piano teacher, an art class taught by the retired curator of the local art institute, and a reading group hosted by a retired third-grade teacher.

Intermittent contact with older adults who share some expertise with the children. Programs, for example, on gardening, baking, and simple carpentry have provided many opportunities for children to learn skills that are quickly becoming outdated and lost.

Intermittent contact with older adults on special occasions such as "grandparents' days" and holiday celebrations. Other special events might include celebrations held in recognition of the Week of the Young Child or National Intergenerational Week.

Unplanned, spontaneous contact with the children's grandparents, who are invited to stop by the childcare center at any time to help feed their grandchildren or to participate in their daily activities and/or care.

On-site child- and eldercare programming in a common setting that can be planned or spontaneous. As an example, the research on which this book is based took place in the McKinley Centre located in Canton, Ohio. This rehabilitation of a former high school opened in December 1984. The developer and the owners of this project knew that they wanted to create a life care center that would include a nursing home, assisted living area, and apartments for elders who were able to live independently. However, there was so much square footage remaining in the building that they looked for feasible suggestions for its use.

A number of consultants were hired to help generate ideas for programs that could occupy available vacant space. One of the recommendations called for the establishment of an intergenerational program—an adult daycare center located across the inner courtyard from a child daycare center. Initially this proposal was turned down, but when resubmitted as two separate proposals, it was accepted. In this new recommendation, the adult daycare center was proposed as an extension of the life care center and the continuum of care concept—a facility that would act as a "feeder" for the other older adult services that had been already planned. The child daycare center was presented as an enhancement for employee recruitment and retention.

It is interesting, however, that funding for the construction of these two centers resulted from a grant proposal, submitted to a community foundation, that emphasized the uniqueness of such an intergenerational center. On-site centers, such as this one, allow for spontaneous interactions, avoid such problems as transportation, and enable staff to have more frequent contact and planning time.

PREPARING THE STAFF MEMBERS

Before attempting to develop another center's or agency's interest in participating in an intergenerational program, both the early childhood and the eldercare staffs must first be committed to and feel comfortable with this concept.

Teachers of young children can lack an understanding of older adults and their environments. Some may express discomfort or uneasy feelings about being in an eldercare environment or may not understand the concept of adult day care.

Wheelchairs, walkers, and portable oxygen tanks are equipment needs of the older adult that may disturb the childcare staff. Because many people have never actually been to a nursing home or to an adult daycare center, their images are based upon fiction seen on television or in movies, or from other kinds of secondary information. Even when preparing to work with community elders, the staff may still express concerns if they think of older adults as moody and/or temperamental. Some concerns that might be addressed beforehand are:

Will the older adults make any inappropriate sounds or movements?
Are the elderly going to be very sick?

As nursing homes, for example, are often perceived as not appropriate settings for the elderly, why would these be appropriate places to bring the children?

Will the older adults attempt to undermine my authority with the children?

Other common concerns among childcare staff members include:

Adequate staff: Administrators and directors may be concerned about maintaining child/staff and elder/staff ratios. Planning ahead for additional staff needs is essential.

Time: Staff members may be concerned about the time commitment required to deal with another program. They may already feel pressed for time to accomplish existing goals and curriculums.

Common concerns among eldercare staff members include:

Noise level: Older adults are often distressed by high-pitched screaming and yelling or other noises that make it difficult to hear the person who is speaking.

Safety: Sudden movements, running, and other types of high activity levels may concern older adults, who often have a problem with balance. Additional concerns are summarized in Table 2, page 96.

Suggestions to Build Staff Understanding

- Arrange for the teachers to visit a nursing home or adult daycare center. Allow them to spend some time with the older adults and with the staff. A staff member from the elder's center could give a tour of the site and answer questions about the types of people they serve; their special needs, if any; kinds of behavior to expect; and any other concerns.

- Visit an ongoing intergenerational program.

- Arrange a meeting with child-care professionals and teachers who are participating in intergenerational programs.

- Order a film on intergenerational programs from such resources as Terra Nova Films, Inc. (See Resources in the Appendix.)

- Hold a dinner or a workshop for the teachers and invite a guest to speak about intergenerational programs. At one of our research sites, staff members at both the child and adult daycare centers were brought together for an all-day seminar with a consultant in intergenerational programming.

- Invite community elders to the preschool for specific programs so that the teachers will become familiar with and comfortable among older adults.

- Use a questionnaire to facilitate teachers' discovery of their personal feelings and attitudes toward the elderly, and the teachers' views of bringing together older adults and children. The results of this questionnaire could be discussed before or during a workshop on intergenerational programming.

- Parents of the children or caregivers of the elders might be willing to speak about residential living for the elderly.

- Training programs can be ordered from agencies such as Generations United and Generations Together (see resources in the Appendix).

- As an introduction to community elders, a health care professional could be invited to discuss normal physical changes that occur during aging.

In general, by spending time with older adults who might be involved in intergenerational programs, staff members will achieve a better understanding of their behavior and gain comfort in including older adults in their professional work with children.

CAPITALIZING ON YOUR RESOURCES: INVOLVING ANOTHER CENTER OR SENIOR VOLUNTEERS

Cultivating another center or agency's or community elders' interest in participating in an intergenerational program takes time and careful planning. Persistence, however, often results in a program that everyone can take pride in "showing off" to parents, members of the community, and funding agencies.

In preparing to contact an eldercare center, remember that the initial contact is important. In gerontology centers, it is often best to contact the activities director or the program coordinator, as these people, rather than the executive director or the director of nursing, are responsible for developing and implementing new programs.

Following an information session concerning the benefits of intergenerational programs, you might ask the other center to join you in visiting an existing program or host a joint meeting with staff members who have participated in intergenerational programs.

Ask your own staff members, parents or other family members, or members of your board of directors if they have any contacts at another center. Acquaint them with your plans and enlist their help in making contacts with the other center.

Questions frequently asked that you might want to prepare for ahead of time include:

- How many children (or elders) do we want to participate in a single session?
- Will we come to your center or will you come to ours?
- Who will arrange for transportation?
- How long will these sessions last?
- What time of day will we meet?
- How frequently will we meet?
- Who will plan the program and be responsible for preparing the materials and leading the program?
- Who will pay for this program?

Because the staff turnover rate in both child and adult agencies is often very high, summaries of meetings and telephone conversations and follow-up letters of confirmation are essential.

Specific suggestions for involving community elders include:

- Contact volunteer organizations such as the American Association for Retired Persons or the Retired Senior Volunteer Program. Ask them if your center could submit an article for their newsletter explaining your program and asking for volunteers.

- Ask staff and members of the children's families to have potential volunteers contact you to discuss ways in which they might become involved in the intergenerational program.
- Prepare a listing of special programs that would enhance the curriculum (e.g., gardening, cooking, or simple woodworking). Contact organizations that might have older adults with these skills, requesting their assistance for a time-limited program.
- Generations Together (see Appendix) has published many research studies outlining the experiences and the effect of employing older workers in child care. Remember that intergenerational programs can include older adults who are not volunteers, but are either employees of the center or are given an honorarium for presenting workshops or special programs.

Planning for any new program takes time and patience. It might take as long as six to eight months of information sharing and planning before the intergenerational program begins. There may be problems and difficulties once the program is in place, but with perseverance these can usually be worked out to the enjoyment of the children, the older adults, and the staff.

A listing of benefits and concerns for staff and administrators can be found in Table 2, page 96.

DEVELOPING AN INTERGENERATIONAL PROGRAM: SETTING GOALS

Although writing goals is often time-consuming and tedious, through this process staff members have the opportunity to develop curriculum ideas, express feelings about working with the elderly (or with the two age groups together), and voice any other related concerns. One of the most important reasons for setting goals before beginning an intergenerational program is to ensure a commitment from the staff. By establishing goals, staff members will define and evaluate their feelings, ideas, and myths about intergenerational programs and their potential meaning and benefits for the children and the older adults.

One childcare center plans to use its intergenerational program goals for continued planning and networking. As they visit other intergenerational sites, these teachers will share their goals with other teachers and receive feedback about the feasibility of their plan. Program goals can also be placed in the center's newsletter so that parents or caregivers can begin to understand the purposes of an intergenerational program.

A rather broad but acceptable goal might be to increase the respect of the children for older adults. In this case, you would know you had succeeded if the children became sensitive to the elders' needs by speaking more loudly or moving more slowly, when indicated. A goal for the older adults might be to relate, show, or teach a skill or craft to the children.

Funding

Goals are often a useful tool in asking for funding, as well. Financial support for intergenerational programs usually has to be shared equally by the centers involved, although sometimes program costs are undertaken by only one agency if that center is, for example, asking community elders to volunteer in its center.

Suggestions for funding are:

• Centers could (a) increase their annual activity fee (if applicable); (b) ask parents for a separate donation for this particular program; (c) sponsor a fund-raiser specifically for the intergenerational program.

• Small community foundations will often give serious consideration to such a unique program. These foundations ordinarily give a maximum of five thousand dollars, with the average grant being one to two thousand dollars. Although this may seem like a small amount, these foundations usually only require a one- or two-page grant proposal.

• Often, intergenerational programs can be funded by a specific source. For example, the local garden society might be willing to fund the cost of a vegetable and flower garden, or a lumber warehouse might give some wood and basic tools to help an intergenerational woodworking program. Our intergenerational art show was given financial assistance by a small donation from a local art institute's educational and outreach fund. The institute was also willing to allow one of its art teachers a few hours weekly to participate in this program.

- Larger foundations that do not usually offer grants to either a child-care center or an adult agency are often intrigued by the concept of an intergenerational program.

- Nonprofit organizations can apply for entitlement funds to support the cost of an intergenerational program assistant. This person might be responsible for preparing the activity materials, assisting with transportation, and helping staff members during the program.

- Community organizations are a valuable resource to contact for assistance with funding or with providing volunteers. Some resources include AARP (American Association of Retired Persons); RSVP (Retired Senior Volunteer Program); Retired Teachers Association; service organizations such as Junior League, Rotary, Jaycees, or the Lions Club; religious organizations; or special-interest groups such as garden clubs or arts auxiliaries. Parents or caregivers who are active members of any of these groups might be willing to serve as your contact person or liaison.

If you have an ongoing intergenerational program and are looking for operating funds or monies for a special project, consider contacting these groups in May or June when they plan budgets and set the calendar of programs and events for the upcoming year. Volunteer to be a speaker for one of their programs or offer a tour of your site. These groups are always looking for interesting programs, and your involvement is a great opportunity to begin the search for funds and/or volunteers.

Transportation

Due to cost and liability, transportation is the single most difficult obstacle to overcome. Although transportation for the older adults may not be so problematic, it is better to have the children come to the elders' center rather than the reverse (see the next section on site selection).

Transportation and the older adult

Transportation available to older adults is related to their living arrangements.

Community elders usually are still driving, have a friend or relative who can bring them to the center, or can take advantage of public transportation services available for seniors.

Adult daycare centers and senior centers usually do not have their own transportation. These centers use contract services to provide transportation—services that are often costly and unavailable for special trips outside their regularly scheduled hours.

On a positive note, long-term care facilities, nursing homes, rest homes, and independent living centers usually have vans that are handicap-accessible and are available for such programs. These facilities are sometimes willing to transport the children from their site to the elders' site, and return the children to their center.

Sometimes older adults will need specialized vehicles with chairlifts and wheelchair seats. Also, elders often dislike being outdoors during the winter. Because they are very concerned about falls, older adults prefer to minimize walking—even to and from any vehicle—whenever snow or ice is on the ground.

Transportation and the young child

Many centers depend on volunteer drivers, if covered by insurance. Although parents might be willing to drive and to assist the teachers, you should be aware that a grandparent might not be the best choice as a volunteer driver. A grandparent who is facing his or her own aging might resist visiting a nursing facility or adult daycare center. Although they might be unable to verbalize these feelings, a grandparent who is suddenly reluctant to volunteer may have realized that facing this potential future is personally too difficult.

Site Selection

Advantages of the childcare center

Special age groups: Older adults often enjoy watching and rocking the infants. This is more easily accomplished in the children's center.

Environmental familiarity: Older adults are sometimes curious about what the children's center looks like; where the children eat and sleep; what kinds of activities are available, and so forth.

Advantages of the older adult center

Decreases the older adult's anxiety: Frail older adults often become concerned about returning to their own center when visiting the children. Sometimes, such concerns as "Will I get back in time for lunch or for my medication?" may be expressed after only a short time. These "worries" affect the childcare staff, who may not always know how to respond to an elder's increasing nervousness. This problem does not occur with community-living elders, who can come and go at any time.

Less confusion: There is less noise and movement in the adult center. The pace of activities is much slower, and the noise level is considerably lower than at the children's center, which makes it more comfortable for the older adult.

Handicapped accessibility: Entryways, hallways, and bathrooms in the older adult center are accessible to handicapped elders. All of the tables are at wheelchair height, and all of the chairs have arms at a height that helps the older adult to lower into and rise from a chair.

PREPARING FOR THE FIRST INTERGENERATIONAL VISIT

Selecting and training the staff members

When a prospective teacher is interviewed, those centers that are considering an intergenerational program or that have an ongoing program should inform her or him. Positive past experiences, fears, or uncertainties can then be brought to light and discussed during the interview.

Selection of participants from the present staff can be based on their past or present experiences with older adults or children; their receptiveness to new ideas; their degree of personal flexibility; and their willingness to learn new approaches to activity programming.

Program Planning

Children and adults can begin to participate in an intergenerational program before they actually meet each other, as a way of "easing into" actual visits. The children can make holiday cards for the older adults or gifts to be used as prizes at Bingo; the older adults in a woodworking group can make toys; or special cookies can be baked and then sent to the children a few weeks or even months before face-to-face meetings occur. Photographs or videotapes can be exchanged so that faces can be matched with names.

Children especially enjoy these preparatory activities:

- Read books such as *Wilfrid Gordon McDonald Partridge* (Fox, 1989), and *My Own Grandpa* (Anderson, 1987) to the children prior to their visits.

- Place "grandma" and "grandpa" dolls in the dollhouse, or purchase grandparent puppets so that these figures can become part of the children's play.

- Place a toy wheelchair and wheelchair ramp in the playhouse. If the toy figure that fits into a commercial wheelchair is a child, a grandparent play figure could be substituted.

- Invite older adults into the center to present a special activity or program.

- Host a grandparents' day and then discuss the similarities and differences between these "grandparents" and the elders you are going to visit.

- Ask the children to bring in pictures of their own grandparents or great-grandparents. The children could share and discuss their personal experiences with grandparents.

Minimal preparation of the older adults is required. They will, however, want to know exactly what they will be doing with the children. An organized and well-planned schedule is very important to them. We suggest:

- If the elders require the use of a cane, a walker, or any other type of device to assist them in maintaining their balance, they will be concerned about a child's sudden movements. It will be helpful to let them know that the children will be learning about the elders' needs before the first visit.
- Include the older adults in the planning of the intergenerational program. Not only do they have good ideas, but any concerns they have will usually surface during the planning process.
- Ask the older adults to decide how they would like the children to address them. The older adults may choose to be called Mrs. or Mr., initially, or they may be immediately comfortable with Grandma or Grandpa. It is important to ask them so that this information can be relayed to the children's teachers.

Suggestions for preparatory activities with parents:

- Parents are usually receptive to intergenerational programs. They often feel that the influence of the elderly is positive and provides their child with a caring relationship during their time away from home. Most child and adult centers relate that parents and caregivers find that intergenerational programs present unique opportunities for their child or elder.
- Parents of infants may have concerns about the safety of their babies when they are with the elders. Assure parents that child and adult staff members will always be present and closely supervising this activity.
- Information about the programs should be communicated to the parents in advance, either through a newsletter, meetings, or any other means of communication used by the center.
- A sample permission form can be found in the Appendix.

Planning the First Visit

The first exchange between the older adults and the children is special, so it should be planned jointly by representatives from both centers if another center is involved.

We suggest a group size of eight to ten participants with four to five children and four to five elders. This allows staff members to carry out comfortably an activity program that encourages relationships between members of both age groups. This is a maximum number for a group activity, unless the program is some type of special entertainment, such as a visit from a childrens' zoo.

A group size that has worked very well for us is three children and three older adults. This is an especially effective group size for new programs because the staff can become familiar and comfortable with those problems unique to either elders or children. A total group size of six also seems to build more intimate and long-lasting relationships among all the participants.

At least two staff members are required. It is helpful to have at least one person from the childrens' center and at least one person from the older adults' center.

Forty-five minutes is enough time for a visit that is neither too tiring for the older adults nor too long for the children.

Time of day is an important consideration. Both age groups appear to do better in the morning, especially the older adults, who tire easily in the afternoon.

Day of the week is also a factor. Tuesday, Wednesday, and Thursday are best, because Mondays and Fridays are "transitional days" that seem to be less flexible for the elders, the children, and the staff.

Establish a schedule of who will be responsible for planning the activity, preparing the necessary materials, providing the snack (if there is to be one), and leading the activity. Many childcare centers prefer to plan programs with activities that are developmentally appropriate for the children. However, as we mentioned earlier, members of the elders' staff should be consulted.

Develop an alternate program in case the leader is ill, the children and/or the older adults are not enthusiastic about the original activity, or the weather is not conducive to the activity.

A telephone call early in the morning to confirm that day's program is helpful to ensure that all program materials, staff, and participants will be ready.

Encourage participants to use the bathroom, already familiar to them, in their own center before leaving to visit the other site.

A Typical Schedule

10:00 to 10:10—Arrival. Time for nametags to be given out and greetings to be exchanged

10:10 to 10:30—Planned activity

10:30 to 10:35—Cleanup and preparation for snack

10:35 to 10:50—Snack time

10:50 to 11:00—Departure

Arrival

Having the older adults seated when the children arrive encourages calm among the adults and relieves any anxiety an older adult may have about children making sudden and spontaneous movements.

Nametags that have the first names of the children, the names of the older adults as they wish to be addressed, and the names of the staff members should be provided. Nametags are especially helpful during the first few meetings for staff members who are struggling to learn the names of the members of the other group and their staff. The names should be in large, easy-to-read letters written in black ink on a light background.

Older adults tend to be punctual and expect others to be on time, too. Given the nature of children and the time and effort required to prepare and transport a group of children, these groups are often less punctual. Because it is important to the older adults that the children arrive on time, the preschool teachers must allow enough time so that they will arrive when expected. If there is an unexpected delay, the adult center should be notified as soon as possible.

Planned Activities

We recommend that the initial activities be structured and fairly simple, especially for the first visit. Decorating cupcakes or making glittered macaroni necklaces are projects that provide needed boundaries for both age groups.

Once the staff members begin to feel comfortable with each age group and have gained a better understanding of the capabilities and needs of both groups, the activities can become more complex.

Decide in advance whether the activity will result in a product that everyone will be able to keep. For example, one center chose to have play dough available for its intergenerational program. This seemed like an excellent idea, because each group liked to work with it. However, at the end of the activity, the children's staff told the children to return their play dough to its container, as the children would do at their own center. The older adults, however, wanted to keep their play-dough objects and were upset with the children's staff members, who suggested that they put the objects away. When the older adults emphatically disagreed, their staff members responded passively because they did not want to contradict the children's staff. The issue was finally resolved, but this experience illustrated the need for the staffs at both centers to discuss expected behaviors, rules, and procedures before implementing an intergenerational program and before each planned activity.

Another issue to consider is whether a finished product should be shown as an example of what is to be produced in that day's session. Early childhood teachers will often object to this, because it is believed that showing a finished product dampens a child's creativity. The elders' staff might disagree, because the older adults often want to see a sample of what they will be making that day. A compromise might be to show the older adults an example of a finished product before the children arrive.

Encourage both staffs to experiment with the selected activity before the actual program begins. As an example of what can happen if this is not done, consider the actual experience when Color Bingo was chosen for an intergenerational program. The childcare staff knew that both the older adults and the children enjoyed playing Bingo. What they did not realize was that the particular Bingo game they chose would be difficult for the older adults, who were unable to differentiate between blue and purple on the Bingo cards. The elders' staff might have realized this if they had been given the opportunity to review the game in advance.

Analyze the room and the available furniture in advance. If possible, choose a room that can be used exclusively for the intergenerational program. This allows the older adults to decide how the program will be implemented if it is to be held in their center. A separate room also keeps the children from exploring other parts of the adult center, unless planned.

Take pictures during the activity. These photos can be used in both centers when discussing and sharing this day with the children and the older adults. Photos can also be used as part of a future program for parents and caregivers.

Snack

Snacks are obviously not a required part of any intergenerational program, but snack time can provide an opportunity for conversation and relationship building among all of the participants, including the staff members. When the activity is held in the older adults' center, the elders often enjoy a second cup of tea after the children leave. During this time they like to discuss the activity, the children, and their memories, often sparked by the children's presence.

If the older adults will be visiting the children's center, staff should inquire about any special dietary needs of the elders, such as someone who might be diabetic. The elders' staff can assist in planning an appropriate snack.

Some foods enjoyed by both age groups are: peanut butter and jelly; bananas; cinnamon toast or toast with butter; muffins; and ice cream.

Making the snack can become the activity itself. Foods such as no-bake cookies and cupcake decorating are favorite food-related activities.

MAINTAINING RELATIONSHIPS

Effective intergenerational programs are concerned with ongoing relationships, not only between the children and the elders, but also between staff members of both agencies, because they are the ones who initiate the program and find time in an already hectic day to carry out the intergenerational program.

To help maintain relationships between the children and the older adults, we suggest:

- Photographs taken during the visits can be placed in an "intergenerational album" that is available for the children and older adults to look at in their own centers.

- Videotapes of special activities within the center could be shared between visits.

- Projects that the children or older adults have completed could be given to each other and displayed for all to enjoy. For example, drawings the children have made, or a craft or woodworking project (such as a checkerboard) made by the older adult could be exchanged. Drawings that the children and/or older adults have created can be duplicated on a copier and displayed for all to enjoy.

- "Alumni Days" can be held in which children that have participated in the intergenerational program, but have gone on to attend school, are invited back for a special event with the older adults. The elders enjoy seeing the children as they grow and develop, and they continue to take delight in their accomplishments.

You can also nurture positive attitudes toward intergenerational programs among the staff members by:

- Creating a system for providing feedback. Much of the feedback from the children and elders occurs after the activity has ended, and without a way of sharing comments and reactions, staff members can underestimate how much the program means to the participants. For example, in one situation, one child always sat very quietly during the weekly program. Both staffs agreed that the program appeared to be unimportant to her because she seemed so uninvolved. At a parent-teacher conference, however, the child's parents expressed their delight with the intergenerational program and the effect it was having on their daughter. They went on to explain how she talked about nothing else when she came home. The youngest child in the family, this child finally had some unique experiences to discuss during family dinners. Both the childcare staff and the eldercare staff were amazed, and decided as a result to share information with each other and to seek feedback from parents and caregivers on a regular basis.

- Exchanging brief notes following visits that would detail some of the comments made by the children or the older adults after the program had ended.
- Soliciting comments and reactions from parents and sharing them with each center's staff.
- Sharing feedback received by directors. Feedback is often given only to the director of each center, so each director must make sure to share this information with his or her own staff members.
- Exchanging written feedback. Information is often shared at transitional times, such as when the child goes on to school or when an older adult dies. For example, a thank-you note, written by family members of an older adult who had recently died, mentioned how meaningful the intergenerational program had been to their mother. The family was grateful that their mother had been able to participate in this experience. Notes such as these should be photocopied and shared with the children's center.

We found that some methods for sharing intergenerational experiences with parents and caregivers work especially well. You might try the following:

- Reprint, with permission, comments by the children and the older adults in the center's newsletter.
- Place photos taken during the program at the entrance of the center, with explanatory captions.
- Edit and show slides taken during the intergenerational programs during special events such as an open house.
- Invite the older adults to an open house at the children's center to meet the parents, or ask the children to attend an event at the adult center to meet the older adults' families.

PLANNING YOUR INTERGENERATIONAL CURRICULUM

Using a Curriculum "Web"

A relatively new concept for developing a curriculum is the curriculum web. The web is developed by first observing children (and older adults) and documenting their interests and the themes of the activities (Workman, 1993). It is organized by identifying common concepts, then adding or connecting ideas that relate to the theme until a "web" is formed.

Staff members brainstorm by listing as many subheadings and activities as they can imagine would be appropriate for each age group. As the web is constructed, inappropriate or irrelevant concepts are eliminated, leaving only those agreed on by all the intergenerational staff members. The curriculum web is then put into action and adjusted as needed to fit the environment and available resources.

The finished web contains a variety of activities that can be carried out over a variable period of time with children and elders. The most positive aspect of this approach is that the staff feels very involved in developing the curriculum. A sample curriculum web for intergenerational programs can be found in Table 3, page 97.

Choosing Appropriate Activities

Choosing and conducting activities in ways that engage children and older adults can make or break an intergenerational activity program. Determining whether a particular activity matches the developmental levels of the children and the functional abilities of the elders is critical.

Any activity is made up of a number of separate components and operations. For example, a game needs players, rules, and a physical setting to conduct it. A craft requires materials, the mental and physical skills necessary to use them, and directions that must be followed. If the components of an activity are adapted so that they match the needs, interests, and characteristics of children and older adults, the activity will be successful and beneficial for both age groups. For example, Bingo could be adapted for use in intergenerational programs by using animal cards, rather than color cards. These cards would replace the numbered cards that might confuse the children and would not require the older adults to differentiate between similar colors such as blue and purple.

There are many components that can be examined when analyzing an activity, including:

- Skills required for the activity. Examples include:

  Sensorimotor requirements: How much fine or gross movement is required? What degree of balance and coordination is needed? What level of color or auditory perception is required?

  Cognitive skills: Do the participants have enough acquired knowledge and a long enough attention span? Do they have sufficient short-term and/or long-term memory to follow the steps and directions required to complete the activity?

- Structure and rules. How structured is the activity?

- Interactiveness. Does the activity allow for or require interaction with others? A teacher might, for example, consider whether the activity must be completed in small or large groups or whether it could be an individual project.

- Emotional reactions. Could the activity make a participant feel uncomfortable or even threatened? Some childrens' books, for example, are designed to evoke feelings and emotions; and personal stories and/or memories may disturb or frighten a participant.

- Rewards and benefits. Is the goal of the activity for the older adults and children to enjoy the process (intrinsic reward) or to produce an end-product (extrinsic reward)? If a product is made, who will keep it?

- Cultural or generational relevance. Does the activity build on the interests and experiences of participants who belong to a particular culture or generation?

For example, let's assume the group that you are planning for consists of preschool children and frail elders. In reviewing the list of activities recommended for intergenerational programs (see Table 4, page 98) that include frail elders, simple activities are ranked very high. Making walnut shell boats (see Activities) is both a fine-motor activity and simple. It is summer, and the image of making sailboats is appealing, so you decide to analyze this activity. Your analysis might reveal the following:

- This activity requires a high degree of skill by frail elders. However, if certain parts of the activity require skills that the children and elders do not have, the staff can complete them before the program. For example, making the sails and placing them on the toothpicks might require more fine-motor skills than either group could handle, so this part of the activity could be completed in advance.
- A great deal of interaction might be expected as the children and the elders make and sail the boats. However, older adults can be distressed by children's spontaneous and sudden movements. The activity could be adapted to accommodate the frail elders' concerns and need for safety. The boats can be "sailed" in dishpans filled with water and placed on top of tables in an activity room, with older adults and children seated in chairs around the tables.
- Generational relevance might be observed if the older adults are encouraged to share their stories about making sailboats when they were children.

Creating an Activity File

Establishing a card file of activities that are cross-referenced according to category can be of great help in planning any kind of program. One example of a successful format is shown on page 27.

We have followed this format for the activities in this book, which may be duplicated on manila paper or duplicated on plain paper, pasted on 5" x 8" cards, and kept in a file box. Original activities may be written on copies of the blank card on page 42. Teachers should design activity cards and keep records in whatever format reflects their own needs. Although it is initially time-consuming to record and cross-reference all activities on file cards, the process saves time and effort overall by providing readily accessible activity information. A card in the front of the box that lists the activities in order can also save time.

```
┌─────────────────────────────────────────────────────────────┐
│                      ┌──────────────┐                        │
│   ❁      ❁       ❁   │   CLAPPING    │  ❁       ❁      ❁    │
│                      │    RHYMES     │                       │
│                      └──────────────┘                        │
│                                                               │
│   CATEGORIES:   xxxxxxxxxxxxxxxxxxxxxxxxxxxxxxxxxx            │
│   DURATION:     xxxxxxxxxxxxxxx                               │
│   MATERIALS:    xxxxxxxxxxxxxxxxxxxxxxxxxxxxxxxxxxxxxxxxxxxx   │
│   ..........................................................  │
│   xxxxxxxxxxxxxxxxxxxxxxxxxxxxxxxxxxxxxxxxxxxxxxxxxxxxxxxxxxx   │
│   xxxxxxxxxxxxxxxxxxxxxxxxxxxxxxxxxxxxxxxxxxxxxxxxxxxxxxxxxxx   │
│   xxxxxxxxxx                                                  │
│   xxxxxxxxxxxxxxxxxxxxxxxxxxxxxxxxxxxxxxxxxxxxxxxxxxxxxxxxxxx   │
│   xxxxxxxxxxxxxxxxxxxxxxxxxxxxxxxxxxxxxxxxxxxxxxxxxxxxxxxxxxx   │
│   xxxxxxxxxxxxxxxxxxxxxxxxxxxxxxxx                            │
│                                                               │
│   xxxxxxxxxxxxxxxx                                            │
│   xxxxxxxxxxxxxxxxxxxxxxxxxxxxxxxxxxxxxxxxxxxxxxxxxxxxxxxxxxx   │
│   xxxxxxxxxxxxxxxxxxxxxxxxxxxxxxxxxxxxxxxxxxxxxxxxxxxxxxxxxxx   │
│   xxxxxxxxxxxxxxxxxxxxxxxxxxxxxxxxxxxxxxxxxxxxxxxxxxxxxx       │
└─────────────────────────────────────────────────────────────┘
```

GOALS OF THE MCKINLEY CENTRE INTERGENERATIONAL RESEARCH PROJECT

One of the goals of the McKinley Centre Intergenerational Research Project has been to identify those factors and programmatic procedures that make an intergenerational program successful. The primary focus of this particular research project was to find and publish those activities that are fun for both generations. Too often, well-intentioned eldercare and childcare professionals assume that just mixing older persons and young children in "any amounts" and "doing any activity" will produce positive results for both seniors and children.

This research was conducted jointly by the McKinley Centre Intergenerational Project Director and team members, faculty, and students from the Family Studies and Gerontology programs, Kent State University. We tested the activities with preschoolers and three groups of elders—frail elders, Alzheimer's elders, and community elders. Additional information on this intergenerational partnership, the research site and methods, and the empirical data can be found in the Appendix.

OBSERVATIONS RECORDED AT THE MCKINLEY CENTRE

Frail Elders and Preschoolers

During the twelve-week periods, members of the research team made the following observations:

Frail elders felt a great responsibility to make every activity educational for the children. They often reminded the staff that when they were young mothers there weren't any preschools or nursery schools. As mothers, they were solely responsible for preparing their children for school—for ensuring that they, for example, could print their names and recognize basic colors and shapes. Given this viewpoint, free-form activities such as clear-plastic-wrap painting and stained-glass collages were thought of as fun, but wasteful of the children's time. Instead, the elders wanted to structure activities to include an educational component. For example, when drawing a country scene, the elders asked that the children draw specific animals that would then be identified and described.

The older adults objected to any adaptation of an activity to meet a child's developmental level. Changing the rules at Bingo, for example, so that the children could win more easily, evoked a strong response from the elders. They stated that we made things too easy for the children: "We should maintain the rules, teach them, and encourage them so that they will learn and grow." This viewpoint was also expressed when the children were allowed more physical freedom during activities such as circle games and rhythm band. The elders commented, "In my day, children, when indoors, were always taught to sit up, not allowed to crawl on the floor, and not allowed to move about wildly."

The frail elders enjoyed events that allowed them to participate in activities thought "not proper for an old lady." Activities such as blowing bubbles and visits from the Humane Society and the Zoomobile were greeted with great enthusiasm. "The children give me an excuse to be a kid again. After all, an old lady blowing bubbles or petting a snake would look silly; people would laugh at me."

Activities such as planting flowers would bring back memories of the elders' own homes and gardens, which they had cared for and tended to as young men and women. They shared these remembrances with the children, but more eagerly with each other, swapping tales of the "most beautiful garden in the neighborhood."

The older adults enjoyed participating in many of the craft activities. At times, however, they seemed more interested in completing their own craft than in assisting the children. Those female elders who had children of their own helped the children with their projects, concentrating primarily on the children's needs. Female elders who were not mothers, however, tended to concentrate primarily on their own projects.

Activities that the older adults volunteered to lead were received enthusiastically by both the children and the older adults. Two of the elders who had been teachers volunteered in both sessions to read to the children. In fact, they asked to be given the books prior to the group time, "in order to be prepared." One of the older women who had been sullen and withdrawn since moving into the apartments had reluctantly agreed to participate in the intergenerational program. It was in this same manner that she volunteered to be a reader for the children. However, she discovered that she could hold the children's attention for twenty minutes, encouraging them to ask questions about the story and to share their personal experiences with her. Following the activities, she wrote letters to her family who lived out of town and telephoned those who lived nearby, announcing, "I've still got it! I haven't lost my touch!" This older woman has continued to participate in our intergenerational programs in addition to becoming a floor leader and librarian in the McKinley Centre Independent Living area.

Slower-paced activities that could be accomplished with relative ease allowed for more interaction and conversation between the children and the frail elders. Examples of these are a rote activity such as stringing glittered macaroni and a small-group activity like decorating cupcakes.

"Reminiscing" activities were extremely popular. The director of the S.A.R.A.H. Center collected items from the past such as hats, white gloves, compacts, and glass globes used as insulators on telephone poles. These items evoked many memories and spontaneous actions by the elders, who would often "dress up", break into song ("In Your Easter Bonnet"), or relate stories of their youth to the children.

Crafts that started with a blank piece of paper presented a unique problem. The older adults wanted to fill the entire paper, whatever its size, leaving no blank or "empty" spaces. However, when the paper was too large, an activity became too tiring and boring for the children. Small sheets of paper no larger than 9 by 12 inches seemed to work best.

The older adults were proud of the influence they were having on the children. Whenever the elders noted the children's progress, such as being more communicative or learning a new skill, they always mentioned it during their evaluation time.

The children's teachers observed that the children, without prompting, were "better behaved" when they were with the older adults. During the evaluation, one of the children remarked, "Sometimes when you're with the grandmas and the grandpas, you have to think—you just can't do the activity." When asked what she needed to think about, she replied, "Why, being polite."

Relationships that were formed in the weekly intergenerational group sessions continued informally. These friendships were a source of great pleasure for the elders. For example, one of the older women proudly told the group that when she had seen one of the children the day before in the courtyard, the child called out her name with delight and came running toward her to say "hello" and give her a hug.

Elders with Alzheimer's Disease and Preschoolers

The Alzheimer's elders recognized, at times, that they were less able than the children to participate in some of the activities, and they found this distressing. They would remark that they could remember doing such things as blowing bubbles when they were children, but now as adults they could not remember how to pucker their lips in order to blow the bubble liquid.

The decreased capacity of the elders disturbed the children. For example, when making pinecone bird feeders, one of the adults, much to the wide-eyed amazement of the children, tried to eat the finished product, even after repeated explanations. In these kinds of situations, role reversal was often observed; the child would kindly instruct the elder that she shouldn't be behaving in a particular way.

Also, when the staff explained procedures and the adults did not comply, the children would become confused and ask, "Why don't they listen?" The children were soon aware that there was a double standard operating on the part of the teachers and directors, especially when they noticed that the Alzheimer's elders were allowed to break rules that they had to follow.

One result of the children's frustration was that they would often simply do the activity for the elder when they realized he or she didn't understand. Overall, what we failed to consider was that many of the rules that the children's staff consistently applied could not be applied to the Alzheimer's elders.

The most successful sessions were those that made few demands of the elders, regardless of the kind of activity. An unstructured activity, such as listening to music or watching electric trains, was enjoyable for everyone. Blowing bubbles, however, was frustrating for those elders who attempted to blow the bubbles. Those who chose merely to watch the children blow bubbles outside seemed to enjoy it immensely.

Waiting was often a problem for the Alzheimer's elders. Waiting for a turn at an activity often led to restlessness or wandering.

Activities were originally planned to last from twenty to thirty minutes to match the length of the frail elders' sessions. After a few meetings, however, the research team and staff decided that activities should last no longer than fifteen minutes.

The preschool director and teachers felt that they were inadequately prepared to work with Alzheimer's elders in a structured setting, even though they had participated in a one-day workshop on intergenerational programs that included information on how to interact with elders.

In the activity sessions, the childcare staff had direct contact with the Alzheimer's elders. They had to answer their questions, they had to respond to their confusion and bewilderment, and occasionally they had to help manage their behavior. The teachers often felt uncomfortable and uncertain: "I could work with the frail elders with no problems, and when I've interacted with the Alzheimer's elders (in the adult daycare center) I thought I did okay—what happened?"

Alzheimer's elders do have special needs that must be taken into consideration. Unstructured visits with Alzheimer's elders did not present the same problems for the teachers; without a planned activity, the Alzheimer's elders asked fewer repetitive questions and were less likely to wander. If you decide to include Alzheimer's elders in your intergenerational groups, decide in advance what role each staff member will play, how wandering and other types of behavior will be handled, and how children will be prepared so they will not be confused by the behavior of this group of older adults.

Community Elders and Preschoolers

Elders who were functioning independently and maintaining their own residences in the community—"community elders"—were also invited to participate in our research program. Notices were published in newsletters such as the *Retired Senior Volunteer Project Monthly,* and announcements were made at meetings such as the Stark County Council on Aging. McKinley Centre staff members also invited family members and friends to participate.

However, as the starting date approached, there were not enough senior volunteers. In spite of recruitment efforts, the research team found that community elders hesitated to make a twelve-week commitment, and many needed travel reimbursement. After the Roberta Chamberlin Foundation approved funds for travel reimbursement, enough elders volunteered to participate. They, too, had special characteristics and needs:

The elders insisted that the staff discuss the planned activities with them approximately two weeks in advance to receive their input. The elders took great pride in enhancing activities. For example, when the activity was water play, the older adults suggested dolls and a small washboard, in addition to having toys available such as boats, measuring cups, and funnels.

The children were more assertive in expressing their feelings to the community elders than they had been with the frail elders or the Alzheimer's elders. This was particularly true while participating in activities that the children felt did not require the assistance of the older adults.

However, there were times when the children would become passive in response to authoritative, "parental" comments from the older adults. An example of this occurred during a reading session. One elder who had volunteered to be the reader started reading *Boss for a Week.* All the children responded excitedly and happily to her questions about what they would do if they were boss for a week: "I'd eat macaroni and cheese every day," and "I'd make my mommy and daddy buy me pizza every day." In contrast, the next adult leader commented before reading *Just Go To Bed,* "I think that all good boys and girls should go to bed when told. There should be no fuss. Good boys and girls don't act that way." Nods and agreement from the other elders reinforced the reader. The children remained quiet throughout the rest of the session, answering questions in a passive manner.

The community elders liked being actively involved. "I enjoy being busy. Just sitting here without anything to do is no good. The children have to understand and to see that just because we're old doesn't mean that we can't be helpful to them."

Community elders enjoyed helping teachers make decorations for holiday events. Grandmas and grandpas also made wonderful substitute "parents" at events such as Mother's Day teas when parents were unable to attend.

This group of older adults appeared to be the one with which the children were most comfortable. They formed relationships easily and expressed their feelings readily, often with a child sitting on an adult's lap during an entire activity session.

Recommendations

- Recognize that older adults are not a homogeneous group, but are individuals that can have similar characteristics and capabilities. Identifying the abilities of the elders will be important for planning your curriculum.

- Analyze each activity carefully to determine whether the older adults and children with whom you are working will have some success in doing the activity.

- Key features for any activity: it should involve only one or two basic steps, and there should be very few directions or rules. Both older adults and children are inhibited by activities that are highly structured or have too many rules.

- Plan to work with small groups of children and elders or in one-to-one situations for no longer than fifteen to thirty minutes.

- Consider carefully the cautions included in this manual before bringing together preschool children with Alzheimer's elders.

- Train the childcare and eldercare staff so they are familiar with the characteristics of each age group and can lead activities appropriate for both.

- If possible, use the same staff members in each session.

- Prepare the children and the older adults for the interaction by explaining what will take place and why.

- Consider allowing the older adults (especially community-living participants) to be involved in planning activities for children.

- Plan intergenerational programs in which older adults are encouraged not only to interact with children by reading stories, playing games, and working on craft and art projects, but also to share or "teach" vocational and avocational expertise and skills.

We hope that our experiences will prove useful to professionals interested either in developing intergenerational programs or in enhancing ongoing efforts. Our intergenerational activities were highly valued by both children and older adults, but it is important to choose appropriate activities and to be aware of possible concerns when bringing together elders and children. We also hope that our project will serve as a model for intergenerational programs with other age groups of children.

EVALUATING YOUR INTERGENERATIONAL PROGRAM

Although it is helpful to have ongoing evaluations by staff and participants, more formal evaluations could be accomplished in the following ways:

- A questionnaire could be sent once a year to the parents and caregivers to solicit comments and suggestions and to ask, "What intergenerational activities did your child/older adult enjoy the most?" "What activities did she or he enjoy the least?" "What kind of effect do you think this program had on your child/older adult?"
- Staff from both centers could meet twice a year to exchange information, evaluate the program, and set goals. Perhaps each agency could pay for an annual dinner so this could be combined with some social time.
- A questionnaire could be sent to any elder involved in the program (see Appendix).
- The program evaluation forms found in the Appendix can be completed and kept on file. Although they were developed for use in the research project, these forms can be used by teachers, observers, or participants.

REFERENCES

Bekker, L. D., and C. Taylor. "Attitudes toward the aged in a multigenerational sample." *Journal of Gerontology* 21:115–18, 1966.

Foster, R. *Children's reactions to intergenerational programs in a long-term care facility.* Manuscript, 1993.

Goodman, B. "Portrait of Maria." In *Voices—Bridging the Gap,* edited by J. Ranahan and A. Griff. Cleveland: Nord Family Foundation, 1993.

Kocarnik, R. and J. J. Ponzetti. "The influence of intergenerational contact on child care participants." *Child Care Quarterly* 12:244–50, 1986.

Lyons, C. "Interagency alliances link young and old." *Children Today* 15(5):21–25, 1986.

Newman, S. *Creating effective intergenerational programs.* Pittsburgh: Generations Together, 1986.

Reville, S. "Young adulthood to old age: Looking at intergenerational possibilities from a human development perspective." In *Intergenerational programs: Imperatives, strategies, impacts, and trends,* edited by S. Newman and S. W. Brummel. New York: Haworth, 1989.

Speert, T. "And now I buy green bananas." In *Voices—Bridging the Gap,* edited by J. Ranahan and A. Griff. Cleveland: Nord Family Foundation, 1993.

Waters, R. "Young and old alike." *Parenting* (Oct):74–79, 1991.

Workman, S. "Curriculum webs: Weaving connections from children to teachers." *Young Children* 48 (2):4–9, 1993.

Section 2:
PROGRAM ACTIVITIES

One of our goals at the McKinley Centre has been to publish those activities that worked best in our intergenerational program. The result is this resource of successful intergenerational activities, which features these categories of skills:

Cognitive: These activities require the use of some cognitive abilities such as recall or memory, classification, or logical reasoning.

Generational: These activities incorporate some aspect of the older generation's culture and prior nationality or the young child's culture and family nationality.

Fine Motor: These activities help the children and elders practice small hand movements and improve their coordination.

Gross Motor: These activities encourage children, and any elders who are capable, to move their large muscles. They also allow for passive participation by any elders who are unable to move about freely among children.

Long-Term: These activities require that children and elders meet repeatedly over a period of time in order to complete a project.

Passive: These activities require only the passive company of children and elders together. They may be primarily focused toward the interest of one group, but should offer something of interest to both groups, if possible.

Process: These activities emphasize the process of working together rather than any end product.

Product: In these activities, emphasis is placed on the end result rather than the process. Painting, for example, becomes a product activity rather than a process activity when participants are requested to paint a particular picture with specific objects.

Projective: These activities allow children or elders to express their feelings vicariously through art, theater, literature, or another expressive medium.

Rote: These activities require repetitive words or motions, usually from memory. Rote performances seem to satisfy the children's love of repetition and the elder's more stable long-term memory.

Short-Term: Any appropriate activity that is completed within one session.

Simple: These activities have few directions, steps for completion, or specific requirements.

Structured: These activities have some structure in that directions must be given and followed.

To make the most out of the activity guide that follows, you might want to define your program according to the capabilities of your older adults (see Table 4, page 98). For example, although long-term activities may have been rated highly by preschoolers and Alzheimer elders, such activities as Weather Watchers may demand higher level cognitive skills than an Alzheimer elder may possess and thus would be inappropriate. Find an activity that would appeal to your group of elders, then turn to the detailed description in the alphabetically arranged guide.

These activities worked especially well with **frail** elders and preschoolers:

Gross Motor
Beanbag Make and Toss
Bluebird Game
Everybody Do This
Indoor Snowmen
Rhythm Band
Simple Exercises
Water Play

Simple
Crayon on Sandpaper
Grass and Flower Paint
Silly Putty
Snow Collages

The following activities were well received by **Alzheimer's** elders and preschoolers:

Gross Motor
Beanbag Make and Toss
Bluebird Game
Everybody Do This
Indoor Snowmen
Rhythm Band
Simple Exercises
Water Play
Working with Wood

Long-Term
Homemade Beads
Leaf Stained Glass
Mailboxes
Spring Village

These activities received high ratings from **community** elders and preschoolers:

Cognitive
Adaptive Bingo
Button Box Sorting
Button, Button, Who Has the Button?

Concentration
Feel Box Prints
Stringing Cereal

Generational
Bubble Blowing with Wooden Spools
Flags and Food Galore
Going Fishing
Hatbox Memories
"Mashed Potato" Fingerpaint
Shaving Cream Painting

Passive
Dentist Guest Speaker
Pet Show
Petunia

Projective
Face Collage
Foil Figures
Paper Dolls
Puppet Play

Process (if not directed)
Clay
Cook and Bake
Painting
Sand Play
Water Play

Rote
Clapping Rhymes
Doggie, Doggie, Where's Your Bone?
Lacing Foam Pictures
London Bridge
One Potato, Two Potato
Singing
Stringing Cereal

Structured
Eggs with Pressed Flowers and Leaves
Paper Plate Animals
Performances and Storytelling
Popcorn Tree

ACTIVITIES

Activity	Categories	Page
Adaptive Bingo: "Raisins in a Line"	cognitive, structured, complex	43
Bean Bag Make and Toss	process, long-term, gross motor	44
Bluebird Game	gross motor, rote, structured	44
Bottle Sculpture	fine motor, unstructured	45
Bubble Blowing with Wooden Spools	active, generational, unstructured	46
Button Box Sorting	cognitive, structured, generational	47
Button, Button, Who Has the Button?	cognitive, fine motor, generational	47
Clapping Rhymes	generational, gross motor, rote	48
Clay	process, fine motor	49
Concentration	cognitive, structured, generational	50
Cook and Bake	process, short-term, fine motor	50
Crayon on Sandpaper	simple, process, generational	51

ACTIVITIES

Activity	Categories	Page
Dentist Guest Speaker	passive, generational	51
Doggie, Doggie, Where's Your Bone?	active, structured, rote	52
Eggs with Pressed Flowers and Leaves	structured, fine motor	52
Evaporation	long-term, process	53
Everybody Do This	gross motor, process	53
Face Collage	projective, process, cultural	54
Fantasy Collage	fine motor, unstructured, projective	54
Feel-Box Prints	generational, long-term, structured	55
Flags and Food Galore	generational, structured	56
Foil Figures	process, unstructured, fine motor, projective	56
Going Fishing	generational, structured, cognitive	57

ACTIVITIES

Activity	Categories	Page
Grass and Flower Paint	simple, process	58
Hatbox Memories	generational, process	58
Homemade Beads	long-term, product	59
Indoor Snowmen	gross motor, generational	60
Lacing Foam Pictures	rote, simple	60
Leaf Stained Glass	long-term, active	61
London Bridge	rote, active, gross motor	62
Mailboxes	long-term, process, generational	62
"Mashed Potato" Fingerpaint	process, fine motor	63
One Potato, Two Potato	rote, active	64
Painting	process, fine motor	65
Paper Dolls	projective, simple	65

ACTIVITIES

Activity	Categories	Page
Paper-Plate Animals	structured, product	66
Performances and Storytelling	structured, process, active	66
Pet Show	passive, cognitive	67
Petunia	passive, projective, generational	67
Play-Dough Sculpture	unstructured, generational	68
Popcorn Tree	structured, simple	68
Puppet Play	projective, generational, cultural	69
Rhythm Band	gross motor, process	69
Sand Play	gross motor, process	70
Shaving Cream Painting	generational, unstructured, process, projective	70
Silly Putty	simple, process, long-term	71

ACTIVITIES

CATEGORIES:

DURATION:

MATERIALS:

ADAPTIVE BINGO: "RAISINS IN A LINE"

Categories: Cognitive, Structured, Complex
Duration: 30 minutes
Materials: "Bingo Cards," raisins, 9 small cards with a single digit on each card, a hat

....

Make as many Bingo cards as needed with the numbers 1–9 placed randomly on nine squares as shown on Card 2. Have nine smaller cards, each with one number, that can be used for drawing out of a hat. Have the children practice pointing to the correct numbers as they are called out. Also have the children practice making lines with their fingers, across and down the rows of numbers so they understand "in a line." Each person will take a turn drawing a number out of the hat. Throughout the game, the elders can help the children find the correct numbers as well as identify "raisins in a line."

Card 1a

ADAPTIVE BINGO: "RAISINS IN A LINE"

Continued from Card 1a

....

When someone calls out "Raisins in a line," all players get to eat the raisins on their cards, and the next game begins.

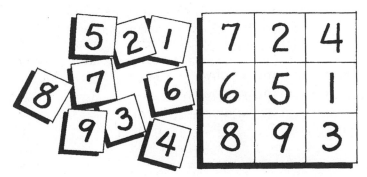

Card 1b

BEANBAG MAKE AND TOSS

CATEGORIES: Process, Long-term, Gross Motor

DURATION: 20 minutes

MATERIALS: 2 or 3 lbs. assorted dried beans and peas; several (clean) old socks

....

Let children and elders make beanbags by selecting beans (dried limas, brown beans, northern beans, peas, etc.) and putting about a cupful in the toe of an old sock. Bean selection will give the elders an opportunity to tell the children the various characteristics and uses of the dried beans and peas. (Some dried beans or peas could be soaked in water overnight to see what happens and then perhaps cooked and eaten. Dried beans from the grocery will usually sprout and grow, too, so some could be used this way.) When the dried beans have been placed in the toe, tie a knot in the sock and leave part of the top for a "handle." Let children and elders toss the beanbags into strategically placed buckets, through holes cut in cardboard, or at a target on the wall.

Card 2

BLUEBIRD GAME

CATEGORIES: Gross Motor, Rote, Structured

DURATION: 10 minutes

MATERIALS: None

....

Elders stand (or some may be in wheelchairs) in a circle holding hands. All but two children join the circle as well. The two "bluebirds" weave in and out the "windows" formed by the gaps under the outstretched hands while all sing:

Bluebirds, bluebirds, go through my window,
Bluebirds, bluebirds, go through my window,
Bluebirds, bluebirds, go through my window,
Oh, bluebirds, aren't you tired.

Card 3a

BLUEBIRD GAME

CONTINUED FROM CARD 3A

....

Pick another child and tap her on the shoulder,
Pick another child and tap her on the shoulder,
Pick another child and tap her on the shoulder,
Oh, bluebirds, aren't you tired.

During the second verse, the two children who began pick other children to be the "bluebirds" and the game is repeated. Any elders who are capable may join the category of possible "bluebirds" and the song changed to "pick another grandma" or "pick another grandpa."

Card 3b

BOTTLE SCULPTURE

CATEGORIES:	Fine Motor, Unstructured
DURATION:	30 minutes
MATERIALS:	Plastic bottles, wallpaper paste, water, scissors, newspaper, scrap materials, glue, paint, smocks
VARIATIONS:	Make a large container by cutting a plastic gallon jug in half. Make a small container from a six-ounce juice container.

....

Prepare ahead one cup wallpaper paste mixed with one cup or more of water to make a watery glue; newspaper or other lightweight paper cut into strips one inch wide; clean plastic soda bottles; and small scraps of fabric, foil, felt, or colored plastic wrap. Encourage children and elders to dip the paper and scraps in the glue and press them onto the outside of the bottle. Allow to dry until the next session, then paint with liquid tempera, if desired. Smocks should be used to protect clothing.

Card 4

BUBBLE BLOWING WITH WOODEN SPOOLS

CATEGORIES: Active, Generational, Unstructured
DURATION: 20 minutes
MATERIALS: Ivory® soap, wooden spools, water, bubble mixture and wands, if desired

(This activity is fun for children and elders to do in pairs.) Provide each participant with a bar of Ivory soap, a small pan of water, and a wooden spool. Before the bubble-blowing wand was invented, our grandparents blew bubbles through wooden spools; now they are delighted to show children how it works. Let elders show the children how to moisten the soap and one end of the spool, rub the spool on the soap, and blow gently though the other end. Extend the activity by providing a small cup with commercial bubble medium and wands, or make your own bubble mixture by combining equal parts of Dawn® dishwashing liquid and water and allowing the mixture to sit overnight.

© Addison-Wesley Publishing Company, Inc.   Card 5a

BUBBLE BLOWING WITH WOODEN SPOOLS

CONTINUED FROM CARD 5A

This activity may be done indoors with just the soap and spools, but perhaps should be moved outdoors if wands and bubble mixture are added. Be careful to do it in a carpeted area indoors; bare floors can become slippery if the bubble solution is spilled.

© Addison-Wesley Publishing Company, Inc.   Card 5b

BUTTON BOX SORTING

CATEGORIES: Cognitive, Structured, Generational

DURATION: 15 minutes

MATERIALS: Button collections (possibly the elders' own collections), six-cup muffin tins. Extension materials: manila or construction paper, markers, glue in small bottles, and/or pipe cleaners

....

Have children and elders work in pairs. Provide each pair with a collection of old buttons and a muffin pan with six cups. Elders encourage the children to classify the buttons into related, logical categories and place them in the muffin tins. If there are as many cups as classes, make an "other" category. Encourage reclassification as well. The activity could be extended by allowing the children to choose five buttons to glue on the outline of a coat drawn on construction paper or to choose one button to make into a "ring." Put the button of choice on a two-inch length of pipe cleaner and twist to finger size.

Card 6

BUTTON, BUTTON, WHO HAS THE BUTTON?

CATEGORIES: Cognitive, Fine Motor, Generational

DURATION: 10 minutes

MATERIALS: None

....

Take a minute for everyone to count the buttons on their own clothes and describe them. Provide a large, clear container of buttons for everyone to see. Empty the buttons out of the container and allow the children to examine and "sort through" the collection. They may sort by color and/or size. The elders may discuss sewing, favorite buttons from older clothes, why people save buttons, etc. Then let the group play "Button, button, who has the button?"

Children and elders sit in a circle with right hands held out in fists and left hands palm up. One child or elder is "It." When "It" says, "Pass," everyone pretends to pass (or actu-

Card 7a

BUTTON, BUTTON, WHO HAS THE BUTTON?

CONTINUED FROM CARD 7A

ally passes) the button to the open hand on the right, trying to keep "It" from seeing the button. "It" guesses who has the button. If the guess is correct, the one who has the button becomes "It." If the guess is wrong, the turn is repeated, or a new "It" may be selected after two turns.

Card 7b

CLAPPING RHYMES

CATEGORIES: Generational, Gross Motor, Rote
DURATION: 10 minutes
MATERIALS: None

Children and elders in pairs sit facing each other. To any of a variety of rhymes, participants slap hands on knees, clap hands, and then slap each other's hands—then repeat the sequence. Encourage participants to suggest rhymes. One possibility:

Pease (slap hands on knees) porridge (clap hands) hot (slap other's hands),
Pease (slap hands on knees) porridge (clap hands) cold (slap other's hands),
(and so on through the rhyme)
Pease porridge in the pot, nine days old.

Card 8a

CLAPPING RHYMES

CONTINUED FROM CARD 8A

Some like it hot,
Some like it cold,
Some like it in the pot,
Nine days old.

Card 8b

CLAY

CATEGORIES:	Process, Fine Motor
DURATION:	20–30 minutes
MATERIALS:	Clay, small bowls of water, tools (see below), smocks

Make your own clay by combining 1 cup cornstarch with 2 cups baking soda in a pan; add 1 1/4 cups water gradually and stir over medium heat to desired consistency. Knead well and store in a plastic bag until needed.

Have the children and elders work in pairs. Assemble a variety of tools to work with the clay, such as plastic utensils, string, rolling pins, pastry cutters, and even a garlic press for "hair." Also set out a small bowl of water for each twosome for dipping hands into—the extra water will further soften the clay, and can keep hands somewhat clean during the activity. Provide smocks to protect clothing.

Card 9

CONCENTRATION (MEMORY GAME)

CATEGORIES: Cognitive, Structured, Generational
DURATION: 15 minutes
MATERIALS: Set of 12 to 16 cards, with 6 or 8 pairs of matching pictures

....

Make a set of six or eight pairs of concentration cards for each child/elder pair, or if possible allow the participants to make their own. Provide a wide variety of stickers, rubber stamps, or markers and crayons to draw representative figures on the cards. Polaroid photos of six or eight matching items or scenes of interest to the participants could also make up a set of cards. To play, lay the cards in rows (3 x 4 if twelve or 4 x 4 if sixteen). Players take turns turning over two cards at a time, searching for a match. If a match is made, the player gets a second turn. Whoever ends with the most matches is the "winner," but the emphasis should be on the challenge rather than on winning.

Card 10

COOK AND BAKE

CATEGORIES: Process, Short-Term, Fine Motor
DURATION: 30 minutes
MATERIALS: Recipe, ingredients, cooking utensils; see below for suggestions

....

Children and elders enjoy simple cooking projects. Provide cupcakes for them to decorate, making materials available to create faces. Coconut dipped in food coloring sprinkled at the top for hair; chocolate-covered candies for eyes; chocolate bits, red candy hearts, or candy corn for the nose; and part of a licorice whip for the mouth work well. Let participants create their own designs.

Card 11

CRAYON ON SANDPAPER

CATEGORIES: Simple, Process
DURATION: 30 minutes
MATERIALS: Sandpaper, large crayons, soap, paraffin

....

Provide sandpaper of various textures and cut it into a variety of shapes and sizes. Let the children and elders color on the sandpaper. Provide old (large) crayons, some with the paper removed, for the participants to experiment with different effects. Scraps of soap or paraffin might also be included. The paraffin would give the elders an opportunity to tell the children about its use in sealing jams and jellies.

Card 12

DENTIST GUEST SPEAKER

CATEGORIES: Passive, Generational
DURATION: 15–20 minutes
MATERIALS: Provided by the guest

....

Many dentists or their assistants are willing to come to a care facility to talk about their profession. Encourage them to bring models of teeth, toothbrushes, floss, and other equipment to show as they talk about dental care and hygiene. Inform your guest that elders will also be present and to include care of dentures in the presentation. Children are fascinated by dentures, and both groups will usually remain interested in the other's age-specific needs. Prepare older adults ahead of time to be sure they will not find a discussion of dentures embarrassing. Participation should be optional.

Card 13

DOGGIE, DOGGIE, WHERE'S YOUR BONE?

CATEGORIES: Active, Structured, Rote
DURATION: 10–15 minutes
MATERIALS: Small object for bone

Children and elders sit in a semicircle with one child or elder in the middle as the "doggie." Choose an object that can be hidden in small hands to represent the bone. The doggie sits in the middle with eyes closed (bone under the chair) as the group chants:

Doggie, doggie, where's your bone?
Someone stole it from your home.

During the chant, the leader designates a child or elder to "steal" the bone. The doggie then opens its eyes and has three guesses to determine who has the bone. Choose a new doggie and repeat.

Card 14

EGGS WITH PRESSED FLOWERS AND LEAVES

CATEGORIES: Structured, Fine Motor
DURATION: After hard-boiled eggs are at room temperature, 15 minutes
MATERIALS: Hard-boiled eggs, small pressed flowers or leaves, rubber cement

Make sure hard-boiled eggs are at room temperature. Wipe the eggs with a tissue or soft cloth to remove dust or smudges. Let elders show children how to paint an even layer of rubber cement wherever the leaf or flower is to be placed, lay a small pressed flower or leaf on the wet cement, and gently pat it down until it is glued flat to the egg. Each person may glue down other leaves and flowers on the egg and carefully rub away any excess rubber cement after it has thoroughly dried.

Card 15

EVAPORATION

CATEGORIES: Long-Term, Process

DURATION: One to five days

MATERIALS: Handkerchief, radiator or heat duct, two flat dishes, salt and water

. . . .

Have each pair of children and elders wet a handkerchief and place it over a radiator or heat duct to observe evaporation. Also, using two flat dishes, have them put a mixture of salt and water in one and water only in the other. After evaporation, talk about the residue or lack of residue and taste it.

Card 16

EVERYBODY DO THIS

CATEGORIES: Gross Motor, Process

DURATION: 10 minutes, maximum

MATERIALS: None

. . . .

Children and elders take turns doing some kind of motion for the others to imitate while all sing:

Everybody do this, do this, do this.
Everybody do this, just like _____.

Card 17

FACE COLLAGE

CATEGORIES: Projective, Process, Cultural

DURATION: 20 minutes

MATERIALS: Facial features cut from magazines, manila paper, markers, glue in small individual bottles, yarn, sticky dots, cutouts, as desired

....

Provide a large selection of facial features cut from magazines. These features should be large ones. For each child and older adult, provide the basic outline of heads (ovals) of varying sizes, drawn on manila paper. Encourage each participant to fill in the faces, making themselves, various family members, or other significant individuals in their lives. Yarn for hair, sticky dots for earrings or rouge, cutout hats and glasses, and the like may also be provided to finish the likenesses. Encourage the participants to share information about their "people."

© Addison-Wesley Publishing Company, Inc.   Card 18

FANTASY COLLAGE

CATEGORIES: Fine Motor, Unstructured, Projective

DURATION: 20 minutes

MATERIALS: Paper punch, colored papers, wrapping papers, greeting cards, foil, glitter, scraps of thread, yarn, embroidery floss, clear adhesive-backed plastic sheets (about 12" x 18"), white paper of equal size, if desired

....

Gather materials and place them within easy reach. Encourage children and elders to spend time examining and preparing the materials. For example, provide paper punches so they can make a quantity of small paper circles of various colors; have them tear some paper and foil into small bits, and cut thread/yarn into short lengths. This process will provide the opportunity for elders to talk about how they used the materials, especially if items such as embroidery thread, yarn, and old greeting cards are used.

© Addison-Wesley Publishing Company, Inc.   Card 19a

FANTASY COLLAGE

CONTINUED FROM CARD 19A

Remove the protective backing from clear adhesive plastic and place it on the table sticky side up. Tape the corners to the table. Let children and elders create a fantasy picture. Then remove the tape from the corners of the plastic and either place another plastic sheet over the collage to make a windowlike finished piece or place white paper over the collage. (Turn the collage over to view.) Hang the collage in a window or doorway.

Card 19b

FEEL-BOX PRINTS

CATEGORIES: Generational, Long-term, Structured
DURATION: 15 minutes (two weeks to fade the paper)
MATERIALS: Collection of small objects, feel box or bag, construction paper

Choose a variety of small objects with unique shapes of interest to children (blunt-tipped scissors, ball, crayon, cotton swab) and elders (darning egg, glasses, pipe, handkerchief) and allow them to name and discuss each item before placing it in a feel box or feel bag. Feel boxes can be made from shoeboxes or larger boxes with slit felt over the holes, or a feel bag can be as simple as a pillowcase. Let the children and elders practice identifying the objects by feel, then choose one to make a print. Prints are made by laying the chosen objects on a piece of dark-colored construction paper in a sunny window. Over a period of time (depending on the amount of light and sun) the paper around the object will fade, leaving a print of the object. Flat objects work better than rounded objects.

Card 20

FLAGS AND FOOD GALORE

Categories: Generational, Structured

Duration: 30 minutes

Materials: Construction paper, glue, and a child's atlas

In advance, ask each older adult to identify the country in which they or their parents were born. Then prepare ahead of time the materials needed to make each of the flags representing those countries; for example, stars, stripes, and any other symbols. Have elders and children work in pairs to make the flag of the country identified by that elder. When all the flags are completed, ask each child to display the flag to the entire group and to identify the country it represents. Ask the older adults to share any information or memories they have of that country. The snack served that day is usually ethnic food(s) representing at least one of the countries discussed.

Card 21

FOIL FIGURES

Categories: Process, Unstructured, Fine Motor, Projective

Duration: 20 minutes

Materials: Heavy strength aluminum foil, scissors, permanent markers

Children and elders will enjoy working in pairs for this activity. Have them draw five lines on a square of heavy strength aluminum foil, as shown on Card 2. Then have them cut on the lines with scissors and crumple the middle section into the head, the side sections into arms, and the two bottom sections into legs. They can twist the trunk area and then pose the figure as desired. Let them create other family members and perhaps pets using varying sizes of foil squares or rectangles, and using a permanent marker to make features, if desired. Encourage the children and the elders to make up scenarios with the figures they have created.

Card 22a

FOIL FIGURES

CONTINUED FROM CARD 22A

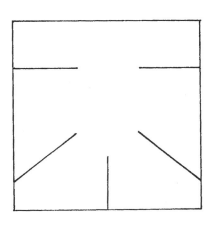

Card 22b

GOING FISHING

CATEGORIES: Generational, Structured, Cognitive

DURATION: 20 minutes

MATERIALS: Sticks, string, small magnets, construction paper fish, crayons, markers, paper clips, dishpans, cookware, and dinnerware, as desired

Cut 5–9 fish from construction paper and place a paper clip on their "mouths." Allow the children and elders to decorate, name, or number the fish, as desired. (Numbering the fish will allow the elders to help children learn to recognize the numerals and give them a sense of purpose.) Provide a stick and a fifteen-inch length of string with a small magnet tied to the end for a fishing pole. Let the children and elders try to "catch" the paper-clipped fish with the pole and magnet. Additional props could include a dishpan for a pond, a frying pan to cook the catch, and dinnerware to "eat" the fish.

Card 23

GRASS AND FLOWER PAINT

CATEGORIES: Simple, Process
DURATION: 20 minutes
MATERIALS: Collection of flower petals, grass and leaves, tongue depressors, paper

Collect a variety of flower petals, grass, and leaves—usually most available in the spring. Let children and elders use tongue depressors to mash the materials onto paper and brush off the excess. This procedure produces a variety of colorful designs depending on the collection of petals and leaves. Red tulips and yellow dandelions make especially bright patterns. Intergenerational discussion may center around kinds of flowers and the smells (as well as designs) produced.

Card 24

HATBOX MEMORIES

CATEGORIES: Generational, Process
DURATION: 30 minutes
MATERIALS: Old hatbox, old-fashioned objects (see below)

Fill an old hatbox with items from the past, such as hats, gloves, an old pocketbook, an old-fashioned handkerchief, lace doilies, a compact, eyeglasses, a perfume bottle, embroidered pillowcases, a tatting shuttle, stockings, a pipe, an old wooden ruler, a shaving brush, old issues of *Look* or *Mechanix Illustrated,* old tools, a pocket watch, old neckties, an old camera with a hand-operated flash, postcards, old valentines, and/or photographs. Tell the group that treasures from long ago are in the hatbox, then allow each person to choose an item from the box. Invite the children to guess what the object is and how it was used, and encourage the elders to share their memories of the object.

This activity was submitted by Debbie Del Corso, Executive Director, Senior Adult Recreation and Health Care Center, Canton, Ohio.
Card 25

CARD 1 OF 2

HOMEMADE BEADS

CATEGORIES: Long-Term, Product

DURATION: One week

MATERIALS: Salt, cornstarch, water, food coloring, nails, yarn

....

The following recipe will produce enough clay for 4–6 elders and children: 2 cups salt, 2/3 cup water, 1 cup cornstarch, and 1/2 cup cold water. Mix the salt and 2/3 cup water in saucepan. Stir and heat for 3–4 minutes. Remove from the heat and add the cornstarch mixed with remaining cold water (with food coloring added if color is desired). Stir until smooth. This clay won't crumble.

Allow a period of free play and experimentation with the clay. At some point, instruct the children and elders to roll the clay into small balls. Have them poke a nail through the center of the beads and set them aside to dry.

Card 26a

CARD 2 OF 2

HOMEMADE BEADS

CONTINUED FROM CARD 26A

....

After a few days, when the balls are completely dry, children and elders can string the balls for a necklace. Different pairs could have different colors of clay and all exchange a few beads so the necklaces would be multicolored.

Card 26b

INDOOR SNOWMEN

CATEGORIES: Gross Motor, Generational

DURATION: 15 minutes

MATERIALS: Clean snow, plastic container or plate, container for snow (such as a bucket), mittens, small containers, strips of colorful fabric trims, buttons, ribbon, raisins, or other decorative items, food coloring if desired

Bring a bucket of clean snow inside. Have children and elders wear mittens, if desired. Let them build a two-snowball snowman in a plastic container or on a plate, containing the ice. They may decorate the snowman with a strip of material for a scarf and add other decorations such as buttons, beans, seeds, sequins or jewelry. For variation, add food items to make snowmen edible. Snow may be sprayed with food coloring and water in a hand-held sprayer for a colorful effect.

Card 27

LACING FOAM PICTURES

CATEGORIES: Rote, Simple

DURATION: 10–15 minutes

MATERIALS: Plastic foam meat trays, pictures, glue, scissors, transparent tape or dull plastic yarn needles (available where sewing notions are sold)

Ahead of time, with a paper punch, punch holes around the edge of several plastic foam meat trays (available in the meat department of most grocery stores or cleaned and saved from home). Holes should be approximately one inch apart and at least one half inch from the edge of the tray. Let children and elders choose a picture from a magazine or their personal supply and glue the picture to the tray. Tie one end of a length of yarn to one hole. The length should be just enough to thread around the tray or even shorter—long

Card 28a

LACING FOAM PICTURES

CONTINUED FROM CARD 28A

lengths are difficult for the children to keep straight and it is better to tie on more than deal with too much. Wrap a short length of transparent tape around the other end of the yarn to stiffen the end, or tie a yarn needle to it. Children and elders may then thread the yarn around the meat tray in a casting over-the-edge fashion or in an over-under style.

© Addison-Wesley Publishing Company, Inc.

Card 28b

LEAF STAINED GLASS

CATEGORIES: Long-Term, Active

DURATION: 15 minutes outside time, 30 minutes at park, 15 minutes inside project time

MATERIALS: Leaves, clear contact paper, scissors, glue, orange construction paper

Let the children and elders collect leaves from autumn trees. (If this activity is planned ahead of time, the groups can go to a nearby park to collect many different kinds and colors of leaves). Have them press the leaves between two sheets of clear contact paper. This forms a colorful autumn collage. Orange construction paper may be used as a border to glue around the leaf collage. This project can be hung on a window to allow light to shine through.

© Addison-Wesley Publishing Company, Inc.

Card 29

LONDON BRIDGE

CATEGORIES: Rote, Active, Gross Motor
DURATION: 10 minutes
MATERIALS: None

....

Have elders hold up their arms to form a series of bridges, either standing or sitting, for children to march under as everyone sings:

London Bridge is falling down, falling down, falling down,
London Bridge is falling down, my fair lady.
(Elders catch a child in their arms on "my fair lady.")

Repeat until each child has been "caught" at least once.

Card 30

MAILBOXES

CATEGORIES: Long-Term, Process, Generational
DURATION: Indefinite
MATERIALS: Boxes or tubes for mailboxes, markers for name-writing and decoration, stickers or other items for decoration

....

Every child (and adult) seems to enjoy receiving mail. Allow children and elders to make and decorate their own mailboxes from shoeboxes, half-dozen doughnut bakery boxes from your grocer's bakery, or 12-inch lengths of large cardboard tubing. Set them up in the room where the elders and children interact. This project may be begun around Valentine's Day, but it is fun to carry it out through the months. Mailboxes can be used at any time children or elders make things they would like to exchange, for small notes of affection or information, and even by the staff for letters of appreciation and encour-

Card 31a

MAILBOXES

CONTINUED FROM CARD 31A

....

agement. Old greeting cards, seasonal holiday cards, thank-you cards, and invitations are all possibilities for use as "mail." Encourage children and elders to produce "mail," and provide opportunities.

Card 31b

✂ -

"MASHED POTATO" FINGERPAINT

CATEGORIES:	Process, Fine Motor
DURATION:	15–30 minutes
MATERIALS:	Ivory Flakes®, warm water, yellow food coloring, mashing or mixing tools, shelf or fingerpaint paper; (optional) cardboard, dinnerware, pototoes, milk, salt, and butter

....

Let children and elders in pairs make "mashed potatoes" the old-fashioned way with a potato masher. "Potatoes" are made from Ivory Flakes, adding warm water slowly and using a potato masher to mix the water and soap. Add a few drops of yellow food coloring and continue mashing until the texture resembles mashed potatoes. This activity will give the elders an opportunity to share with children the items used for mashing before electrical appliances were available. Provide as many types of mixing tools (whisk, egg

Card 32a

"MASHED POTATO" FINGERPAINT

CONTINUED FROM CARD 32A

beater) as possible to stimulate conversation and experimentation. When the mashing process is completed, children and elders may fingerpaint with the mixture on shelf paper, make soft sculptures on cardboard, or pretend play a meal with dinnerware. If desired, provide real cooked potatoes to mash and serve for snack.

Card 32b

ONE POTATO, TWO POTATO

CATEGORIES: Rote, Active

DURATION: 10–15 minutes

MATERIALS: Token for each participant

Children and elders sit in a circle, both hands (in fists) extended with a token (penny, Bingo marker, bean) in one hand. One child or elder is "It" and goes around the circle touching each outstretched fist on the beats of this rhyme (all chanting):

One potato, two potato, three potato, four;
Five potato, six potato, seven potato, more!

On the beat of "More" the hand that is being touched opens up. If there is a token in it, the possessor of the token is "It." If not, the current "It" repeats the process and the rhyme until a token is discovered.

Card 33

PAINTING

CATEGORIES: Process, Fine Motor

DURATION: 15–20 minutes

MATERIALS: Paints, brushes or other utensils (see below), smocks, newspaper, construction paper

Provide watercolors with small brushes, liquid tempera paint with large brushes or sponges, or watered-down food coloring with eyedroppers (eyedropper painting on paper toweling or coffee filters works especially well). Place newspaper under the paper to be painted and provide smocks to protect clothing (liquid tempera will stain less if a drop of dishwashing liquid is added to each cupful). Let children and elders paint, providing opportunity to talk about their paintings. For variety, they could paint on construction paper or over a design that you provide with a permanent marker.

Card 34

PAPER DOLLS

CATEGORIES: Projective, Simple

DURATION: 15 minutes

MATERIALS: Paper dolls (both sexes, different ethnicities, and all ages)

Paper dolls were often played with by the older generations, but are not always available to children today. Provide "old" paper dolls if these can be found, or newer commercial ones, or create your own from manila tagboard. Select sets that include both sexes, different ethnicities, and all ages. Allow children and elders to name their characters and create their own scenes and events with the dolls.

Card 35

PAPER-PLATE ANIMALS

CATEGORIES: Structured, Product
DURATION: 30 minutes
MATERIALS: White paper plates, construction paper, glue, crayons, markers, scissors, yarn

Cut out various legs, heads, tails, ears, etc., from construction paper. Children and elders may then glue these parts to white paper plates (small, large, or both). Provide crayons, yarn, markers, and scissors for special effects.

Card 36

PERFORMANCES AND STORYTELLING

CATEGORIES: Structured, Process, Active
DURATION: 10–15 minutes
MATERIALS: Simple props, as desired, for each story

Elders usually enjoy even the roughest of performances by children. Encourage children to plan and perform such simple and familiar stories as "Goldilocks and the Three Bears," "The Three Billy Goats Gruff," or "The Night Before Christmas."

Elders may reciprocate by telling a story to one to three children in an informal setting, or they may decide to perform a story, much as the children do.

Card 37

PET SHOW

CATEGORIES: Passive, Cognitive

DURATION: 20–30 minutes

MATERIALS: Pets or other animals and their caretakers

....

Invite friends, acquaintances, the local Humane Society, or a pet-store owner to come and share a pet. Cats or kittens are usually a good choice since many elders had or have cats in their homes and children may as well. (Cats are also usually well-mannered.) Fish of various kinds, birds, and well-behaved dogs are also good choices. A pet-store owner may provide more exotic choices such as rabbits, hamsters, or even an iguana. Limit the number to three or four animals each time to provide time for discussion and contact.

A variation of this activity could be the introduction of typically wild animals through a natural resources organization or zoo.

Card 38

PETUNIA

CATEGORIES: Passive, Projective, Generational (depending on video)

DURATION: 20 minutes

MATERIALS: Videotape of children's story (*Petunia* is one example; many others are available from Reading Rainbow Videos, P. O. Box 80669, Lincoln, NE 68501-0669)

....

Borrow the videotape about Petunia, the silly goose who got the barnyard in an uproar when she found a book and became "wise." Show the videotape to the group of children and elders and allow for discussion afterward. Make copies of the book available for rereading by pairs.

Card 39

PLAY-DOUGH SCULPTURE

Categories: Unstructured, generational

Duration: Unspecified

Materials: Flour, salt, oil, food coloring or powdered tempera

....

Participants may prepare the play dough together using the following recipe: 2 cups flour, 1 cup salt, 1 tablespoon cornstarch, food coloring or powdered tempera to color, and about 2 cups water and 3 tablespoons oil to blend. Add food coloring to water before blending, or powdered tempera to dry ingredients before blending. Preparing the play dough with children and elders would provide the elders an opportunity to tell the children about their own experiences with breadmaking or other baking. Then let each person work with a lump of the play dough to make whatever she or he wishes.

Card 40

POPCORN TREE

Categories: Structured, Simple

Duration: 30 minutes

Materials: Glue, construction paper, markers, popcorn, powdered tempera

....

Draw or paint a tree trunk and bare branches on construction paper. Pop popcorn and color it by shaking it in a bag with powdered tempera. Have children or elders glue popcorn on the branches—green with "blossoms" in the spring, or oranges and reds in the autumn.

Card 41

PUPPET PLAY

CATEGORIES: Projective, Generational, Cultural

DURATION: 20 minutes

MATERIALS: Puppets, props, paper and pencil, tape recorder, if desired

....

Provide a variety of hand-puppet figures. Figures might include a variety of animals or a typical group of family members such as mother, father, and children. "Older" puppets (grandmother, grandfather) should be included in the selection if at all possible. A selection of props (combs, toothbrushes, spoons, hats, pencils, etc.) might also be provided to stimulate storytelling or to make the activity more generation-specific. Let children and elders work in pairs to create a story with their puppets. Give them privacy for performing, or encourage them to tape-record or write down their stories, if they wish.

Card 42

RHYTHM BAND

CATEGORIES: Gross Motor, Process

DURATION: 10–15 minutes

MATERIALS: Rhythm instruments (see below)

....

Distribute rhythm instruments such as finger cymbals, triangles, sandpaper blocks, tambourines, and drums to the children and elders. Lead the group in tapping out the rhythm of familiar songs, or get the children and elders to suggest rhythms that all will copy. (If you do this, let each person have a turn.) Avoid rhythm or "marching" sticks, because their use by the children can worry the elders.

Card 43

SAND PLAY

CATEGORIES: Gross Motor, Process

DURATION: 20–30 minutes

MATERIALS: Wet sand in tubs, toys and tools as desired (see below)

Provide wet sand in small tubs that can be placed on tables along with tools and toys such as plastic animals or dinosaurs, measuring cups and spoons, letter-shaped molds, and/or marbles. Allow plenty of free play.

Card 44

SHAVING CREAM PAINTING

CATEGORIES: Generational, Unstructured, Process, Projective

DURATION: 30 minutes

MATERIALS: Shaving mugs, shaving cream, fingerpaint paper, powdered tempera and electric shavers, if desired

Acquire as many shaving mugs and brushes as you need to share among the members of the group. Draw a rough outline of a face on fingerpaint paper and allow the children and elders to mix soap and water in a shaving mug to smear on the face. After a time for experimentation, introduce the shaving cream in a can as the "modern" way, and allow the children and elders to fingerpaint with the shaving cream on the paper. Sprinkle powdered tempera from a salt shaker to color. After cleanup, an electric shaver may be brought out and talked about as one way of shaving.

Card 44

SILLY PUTTY

Categories: Simple, Process, Long-Term

Duration: 30 minutes

Materials: Elmer's® white glue, liquid laundry starch, powdered tempera, objects such as table knives, plastic animals, and toy cars, as desired

Make the following recipe for each 4–6 children and elders: 1 cup Elmer's white glue (other brands do not always work), 1 cup liquid laundry starch, and powdered tempera to color. Mix the glue and laundry starch. Depending on the temperature and the brand of starch, some adjustments may need to be made. If the mixture "beads" into small balls with a skim of starch about, add a little more glue. If the mixture remains in one lump but is tacky to touch, add a little more starch. It is best not to be shy—mix this putty with your hands from the beginning, especially if you double the recipe. Add the pow-

SILLY PUTTY

Continued from Card 46a

dered tempera, if desired, before mixing. The mixture may be made in advance and stored in the refrigerator.

Give children and elders each a lump of silly putty to work with. This material has fascinating qualities. It oozes from hands or over objects. It will not stick to tables or plastic, and it can be used to "lift" print or pictures from newspapers. If it should begin to stick to warm hands, spread a little laundry starch over the hands. It will stick to clothing and must be washed out with warm soap and water before it dries and hardens (Use smocks to avoid contact with clothing.) Provide table knives for cutting, plastic animals and cars to get stuck in the ooze, and objects to hide—you can then watch their forms appear under the putty and guess what they are.

SIMPLE EXERCISES

CATEGORIES: Gross Motor, Structured
DURATION: 15–20 minutes
MATERIALS: None

Children and elders can both enjoy easy movements, especially if presented as a game. Use a format such as "Simon Says" or Hap Palmer's song "Put Your Finger in the Air" to demonstrate the movements. Be sure to lead the activity in a carpeted area that has enough space for free movement, and adapt the game or song to the abilities of your elders. Songs that have a pause between the time the direction is given and the time a response is required work best.

Card 47

SINGING

CATEGORIES: Rote, Generational
DURATION: 10 minutes
MATERIALS: Autoharp or other musical instrument

Children and older adults enjoy singing together for short periods of time, especially if accompanied by an instrument like an autoharp, which is easy to play and helps the group find the key.

Some songs that are usually familiar to both ages are "Rock-a-bye Baby," "Row, Row, Row, Your Boat," "If You're Happy and You Know It," "The Wheels on the Bus," "Eensy Weensy Spider," and "Skip to my Lou." Allow the children and the elders to make requests.

Card 48

SNOW COLLAGES

Categories: Simple, Process, Generational

Duration: 30 minutes

Materials: White flat plastic foam or foam trays, white objects for collage such as cotton balls, cotton swabs, foam cups, rice, navy beans, cupcake papers, doilies, packing foam, tissue, eggshells and scraps of paper; toothpicks and scissors

Gather the materials for the activity and place them within reach. Place the white flat piece of plastic foam or foam tray in front of a child and elder. Tell them to pretend that the white tray is a big field covered with new snow. Let them insert fences, etc., in that field, encouraging them to try many ideas and arrangements before starting to glue down the objects. This activity will give the elders an opportunity to talk with the children about their experiences in snowstorms.

© Addison-Wesley Publishing Company, Inc.   Card 49

Card 1 of 2

SPRING VILLAGE

Categories: Long-Term, Cultural, Fine Motor

Duration: 15 minutes for first day, 20 minutes 4–5 days later

Materials: Drainage saucer for a 10" flowerpot, fresh potting soil, wheat berries or rye grass seed, clear plastic wrap, spray bottle or water, miniature items—toys, figures, animals, eggs, plastic cake decorations

Children can design their own village while nature takes care of the plant life! Fill a flowerpot's drainage saucer with potting soil. Let elders help children sprinkle wheat berries or rye grass seed over the entire surface of the soil. Lightly spray the soil with water until it is damp, not soggy. Cover with plastic wrap to retain moisture. Place in direct sunlight and keep soil moist until seeds germinate (about 4–5 days). After seeds have

© Addison-Wesley Publishing Company, Inc.   Card 50a

SPRING VILLAGE

CONTINUED FROM CARD 50A

germinated, remove the plastic wrap and place the tray near a sunny window. After green sprouts grow, children and elders can create a village setting by lacing small objects in the grass: miniature toys, trees made from twigs, tiny flowers cut from bright tissue paper, and tissue molded from clay. Pathways can be added by clipping the grass. Add miniature bunnies and eggs as Easter approaches, if desired.

Card 50b

STATUE GAME

CATEGORIES: Gross Motor
DURATION: 10 minutes
MATERIALS: Music source

Play the piano or an audiotape or record while the elders and children go through creative motions to the music. Elders may move in their chairs or among the children as desired. Stop the music after a few seconds. When the music stops, the participants "freeze" into statues. Repeat. Choose music that is familiar to and liked by the elders and children in turns. A good album is Hap Palmer's "Homemade Band," which includes the selection "Wildwood Flower," played with "freezing" stops.

Card 51

STRINGING CEREAL

CATEGORIES: Fine Motor, Rote, Cognitive
DURATION: 20 minutes
MATERIALS: Breakfast cereals with large center holes, yarn, plastic yarn needles

....

Let children and elders work in pairs. Give them each their own 24-inch length of yarn with a plastic yarn needle tied to one end and a piece of cereal tied to the other end. From a selection of breakfast cereals with large holes in the middle, participants can make edible "necklaces." To facilitate cognitive development, ask the elders to string in a pattern (i.e., three, two, three, two) and ask the children to duplicate, then extend the pattern. Patterns may vary from very simple to quite complex.

Card 52

VALENTINE TREE

CATEGORIES: Long-Term, Complex
DURATION: 45 minutes
MATERIALS: Branch; small pail; sand or plaster of paris; spray paint; string or yarn; scissors; red, pink, and white construction paper

....

Ahead of time, spray paint a branch from a tree using either white or red paint, place the branch in a pail, and secure it with sand or plaster of paris. Then let children and elders work together as a group to complete this project. Have them cut heart shapes out of red, pink, and white construction paper. They may cut them in different sizes or fold them over before cutting to make a lacy effect. Hang the hearts from the tree with string or yarn. For variety, add other valentine art projects to the tree.

Card 53

WALNUT SHELL BOATS

CATEGORIES: Fine Motor, Simple

DURATION: 20 minutes

MATERIALS: Walnuts, construction paper, play dough, wooden toothpicks, tubs of water or water table

....

Prepare and have available the following: empty walnut shells, small triangular sails, tubs or other containers filled with water so that the boats can be floated when completed, and play dough (to make play dough, mix 2 cups flour, 1 cup salt, and 1 tablespoon cornstarch. Add 2 cups boiling water and 3 tablespoons oil. Add food coloring, if desired.) If desired, the children can crack open the walnuts and remove the nuts at the beginning of the session. Let children and elders place *a small amount* of play dough in the middle of the shell. (Do not use a more elastic commercial product; play dough is easily made and

Card 54a

WALNUT SHELL BOATS

CONTINUED FROM CARD 54A

....

is a better ballast for the "boat.") Have children and elders make a sail by pushing a wooden toothpick through the bottom of a small triangular piece of construction paper and back out at the top. Then they can push the toothpick with the sail into the play dough in the shell, and sail away!

Card 54b

WATER PLAY

CATEGORIES: Gross Motor, Simple, Process
DURATION: 20 minutes
MATERIALS: Water, dishpan, and various items (see below)

....

Provide a dishpan of water for each child/elder pair and a variety of items for experimentation and exploration. Suggestions include food coloring for mixing and making colored water, a doll for bathing, soap, washcloths and towels, a small washboard, cups for measuring and pouring, sieves, sponges, eyedroppers, table tennis balls, and eggbeaters. Let each pair play freely.

Card 55

WEATHER WATCHERS

CATEGORIES: Long-Term, Cognitive
DURATION: Months, 10 minutes each time
MATERIALS: Large thermometers, rain gauges, cardboard thermometers, paper and pencils for recordkeeping, as desired

....

Provide large thermometers mounted outside windows for each group of 4–6 children and elders in the room where they meet, if possible. Have children and elders work in pairs. If desired, provide each pair with a cardboard thermometer made with a red-and-white ribbon to simulate the mercury. Children and elders may match the red ribbon to the number of degrees on the outside thermometer, and/or record the temperature and the date each day they meet. Also provide rain gauges with large numbers (make them larger yourself) for each 4–6 children and elders to measure rainfall.

Card 56

WORKING WITH WOOD

CATEGORIES: Gross Motor, Process
DURATION: 20 minutes
MATERIALS: Scraps of wood, sandpaper, and white glue

．．．

Provide a variety of wood scraps and sandpaper. Encourage the children and adults to examine the kinds of wood by texture, color, and smell. Sanding the wood will help with this examination and it will give the elders an opportunity to share information with children. Let the participants select a base piece of wood and then glue chosen scraps to it as they desire. Glue should be watered slightly and in small individual bottles for ease in handling. Encourage a sculpture for the child and one for the elder.

Card 57a

WORKING WITH WOOD

CONTINUED FROM CARD 54A

．．．

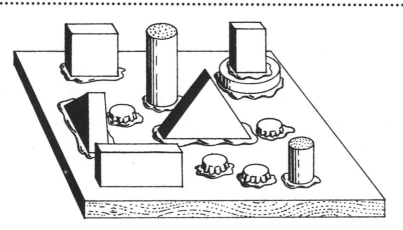

Card 57b

Section 3:
APPENDIX

AN INTERGENERATIONAL PARTNERSHIP

This research project was an intergenerational partnership between the McKinley Centre staff, including the executive director and the directors and staff of the children and adult daycare centers, and the faculty and students from Family Studies and Gerontology, Kent State University.

In this time of decreasing funding and vanishing resources, it was necessary to search for alternative approaches to developing and implementing research. Both sites found many advantages to this arrangement. The Kent State students' internships and field-work in the intergenerational project provided them with meaningful experiences in their profession as they applied theory to actual situations. Students in the gerontology field who were accustomed to working with elders but who may have been hesitant to work with children noted the similarities of developmental principles across the life span and became more comfortable with each generation. Similarly, childcare students learned that caring skills can apply to many age levels, and they too overcame their reluctance to work with people outside their specialty.

The McKinley Centre benefited from the assistance of the students throughout the research. The students' enthusiasm, fresh ideas, and new approaches to problems and clients energized staff members throughout the facility. The research component of the project also created more social contact and involvement for older adults in the center.

The Research Site

The success of the McKinley Centre's intergenerational programs is due in part to the facility in which these programs take place. Built in 1918, the McKinley Centre was once the old McKinley High School—now a historic site in Canton, Ohio. The architectural metamorphosis of this former school has produced a self-contained community encompassing all age groups. In addition to a nursing center, assisted and independent living apartments, an adult day-care center, and a children's daycare center, the center also houses several commercial businesses and the Centre Place Restaurant, which is open to the public. These businesses and agencies open the center and its residents to the community.

Careful attention was given to the planning of the adult day-care center so that it would be close to the children's daycare center. Both centers are handicapped accessible and are located on the same floor surrounding a playground and an outside patio, which are also handicapped accessible. The three-story central atrium, courtyard, and patio all provide shared places for spontaneous interactions as well as for planned meetings. These shared spaces allow the older adults to choose to either interact directly with the children or to watch them from the patio in the courtyard or from benches in the atrium. Often, the sounds and sights of the children, heard from afar, are all an older adult desires.

Research Methods

Description of Participants and Project Cycles

Three types of older adults—frail elders, community elders, and elders who had been diagnosed in the early and middle stages of Alzheimer's Disease—participated in the project. In order to assess the success of activities with each of these groups, four cycles of activities were planned with contact between children and elders twice each week. Each group of elders was to participate in a twelve-week program of activities with preschool children. The twelve-week cycles of activities were to be repeated with each group in order to provide more trials for each type of activity. However, the interaction between Alzheimer's elders and children proved to be problematic, and community elders were recruited to complete the project. This adjustment resulted in four twelve-week cycles of activity programming; two with frail elders, one with Alzheimer's elders, and one with community elders. The elders and children interacted twice a week for a twelve-week period.

Activity Categories

The research team chose twelve paired categories of activities to use with the older and younger participants. This plan resulted in twenty-four types of activities to be done twice a week during the twelve-week cycles:

Structured and unstructured

Complex and simple

Cognitive and rote

Passive and active

Themed (usually holidays) and nonthemed

Process and product

Long-term closure and short-term closure

Fine motor and gross motor

Small group and large group

Culture-bound and nonculture-bound

Generation-bound and nongeneration-bound

Projective material and nonprojective material

Over a period of ten months, with two sessions per week, approximately 80 activities were analyzed. Evaluation of the success or failure of the activities was performed in three ways:

1. By trained observers, who completed an evaluation form during the activity and recorded their observations,

2. By the children, who were asked to evaluate the activity in a room separate from the elders so that they would be comfortable about giving their opinion, and

3. By the elders, who were interviewed as a group by the research team after the children had left at the end of the activity.

The evaluation forms used by the observers can be found at the end of the book. Two members of the research team interviewed each elder and child participant. With the children, it was necessary to use gestures in questioning: "Did you like it this much, this much, or this much?" while expanding the distance between the researcher's held-out arms.

INTERGENERATIONAL PROGRAMMING QUESTIONNAIRE

Recently much attention has been given to bringing together older adults and children for their mutual benefit.

Before developing our own intergenerational program, we would appreciate your opinions on the statements below.

Please indicate the degree to which you feel the following statements are true of young children and older adults when they are together.

1. Children and older adults communicate easily with each other.

    _____Almost always   _____Sometimes   _____Rarely

2. Older adults and children enjoy helping each other.

    _____Almost always   _____Sometimes   _____Rarely

3. Children and older adults naturally feel affection toward one another.

    _____Almost always   _____Sometimes   _____Rarely

4. Children and older adults enjoy each others' company.

    _____Almost always   _____Sometimes   _____Rarely

The behaviors of older persons when interacting with young children and their attitudes toward young children would determine, to some extent, the success of intergenerational programming. Please indicate below the degree to which you feel the following statements are true.

1. Older adults share wisdom with children.

    _____Almost always   _____Sometimes   _____Rarely

2. Older adults are gentle and kind to children.

    _____Almost always   _____Sometimes   _____Rarely

3. Older adults are lenient with children when they misbehave.

    _____Almost always   _____Sometimes   _____Rarely

4. Older adults believe that children should not question their elders.

    _____Almost always   _____Sometimes   _____Rarely

QUESTIONNAIRE (CONT.)

5. Older adults believe that children who receive a lot of attention turn out to be spoiled.

   _____Almost always _____Sometimes _____Rarely

6. Older adults believe in strict discipline for children.

   _____Almost always _____Sometimes _____Rarely

7. Older adults believe that children are basically good.

   _____Almost always _____Sometimes _____Rarely

The behaviors of children when interacting with older adults, and their attitudes toward older adults, would also influence the success of intergenerational programming. Please indicate below the degree to which you feel the following statements are true about children.

1. Children are helpful to older adults who need assistance.

   _____Almost always _____Sometimes _____Rarely

2. Children are willing to cooperate with older adults.

   _____Almost always _____Sometimes _____Rarely

3. Children believe that the older adults cannot do much except passive activities such as sit, rock, go to church, or be pushed in wheelchairs.

   _____Almost always _____Sometimes _____Rarely

4. Children believe that older adults know a lot about a lot of things.

   _____Almost always _____Sometimes _____Rarely

5. Children believe that older adults are friendly.

   _____Almost always _____Sometimes _____Rarely

VOLUNTEER EVALUATION

1. Was this program beneficial for the children?

_____

1   2   3   4   5   6   7   8   9   10
Not at all   *Very beneficial*

Comments:_____

_____

2. Was this program beneficial for you?

_____

1   2   3   4   5   6   7   8   9   10
Not at all   *Very beneficial*

Comments:_____

_____

3. Which activities did you enjoy the most?

_____

_____

4. Which activities did you enjoy the least?

_____

_____

5. Do you have any suggestions for future programs?

_____

_____

6. What could we have done to better assist you while you were here?

_____

7. How did you find out about the program?

_____

_____

8. Do you know of others who would like to volunteer?

_____

_____

Name _____

ACTIVITY EVALUATION

Name of Activity_____ Observer_____

Category of Activity_____ Date_____

Directions: Rate the activity on each characteristic below from Low (1) to High (5). Use (6) for neutral or not applicable.

Introduction	L			H	N/A
1. Could the children understand the directions?	1 2 3 4 5				6
2. Could the older adults understand the directions?	1 2 3 4 5				6
3. Did the children become interested?	1 2 3 4 5				6
4. Did the older adults become interested?	1 2 3 4 5				6

Comments:_____

Process
1. Did the activity hold the interest of the children?   1 2 3 4 5   6
2. Did the activity hold the interest of the older adults?   1 2 3 4 5   6
3. Did the children seem to enjoy the activity?   1 2 3 4 5   6
4. Did the older adults seem to enjoy the activity?   1 2 3 4 5   6
5. Were the children able to follow the directions?   1 2 3 4 5   6
6. Were the older adults able to follow the directions?   1 2 3 4 5   6
7. Did the children possess the skills required for the activity?   1 2 3 4 5   6
8. Did the older adults possess the skills required for the activity?   1 2 3 4 5   6
9. Were the timing and pacing suitable for the children?   1 2 3 4 5   6
10. Were the timing and pacing suitable for the older adults?   1 2 3 4 5   6
11. Did the activity allow for flexibility in process?   1 2 3 4 5   6

Comments:_____

Selection
1. Did the activity match its category labels?   1 2 3 4 5   6
2. Was the activity age-appropriate for children?   1 2 3 4 5   6
3. Was the activity level appropriate for older adults?   1 2 3 4 5   6
4. Are the materials easily available in most settings?   1 2 3 4 5   6
5. Did the activity require extensive preparation on the part of the staff?   1 2 3 4 5   6

Comments:_____

PARTICIPANT EVALUATION

Name of Activity_____ Participant_____

Category of Activity_____ Date_____

As you interview each participant, record their answers on the chart below. In column 1, place a 1 in the box for "not at all," 2 for "somewhat," and 3 for "very much." In columns 2 and 3 answer "yes" or "no." In columns 4, 5, and 6 place an * for significant responses and write their comments and initials below.

Name of child/elder	1 Enjoy?	2 Like to do again?	3 With others?	4 Enjoy most?	5 Enjoy least?	6 Changes?

Comments:

_____

_____

_____

_____

_____

_____

_____

_____

_____

_____

SAMPLE INTERGENERATIONAL PROGRAM PERMISSION FORM

Dear _____

A very important part of the curriculum at McKinley Early Childhood Centre is our participation in the intergenerational program. We have found that this contact between the children and older adults establishes trust between the two age groups, builds self-esteem, and is often the basis for some warm friendships. The children visit the senior citizens on a regular basis, both for planned and spontaneous activities.

The S.A.R.A.H. Center, located on the ground level and across the courtyard from the childcare center, is an adult daycare center. McKinley Life Care is a nursing home located on the second and third floor of the McKinley Centre.

The children are accompanied by teachers from our center each time we visit the seniors. The staff of the centers are also present.

I understand the intergenerational program and acknowledge that a calendar of planned activities is available to me. I give permission for

_____

to participate in all intergenerational program activities.

Signed_____

Date_____

PROGRAM RESOURCES

American Association of Retired Persons (AARP)
1909 K Street N.W.
Washington, D.C. 20049

This organization is committed to helping older Americans achieve and maintain a high quality of life for as long as possible. AARP has developed an interest in intergenerational programs and published a variety of resource materials, including a newsletter issue containing statistical information on the advantages of intergenerational programs.

Center for Family Education
Oakton Community College
1600 E. Golf Road
Des Plaines, Illinois 60016

This intergenerational program offers a three-credit course in intergenerational play.

The Center for Intergenerational Learning
Temple University
1601 N. Broad Street
Philadelphia, Pennsylvania 19122

This center has developed many model projects, including a mentoring program for vulnerable youth. It publishes a newsletter entitled *Interchange.*

Center for Understanding Aging, Inc.
P.O. Box 246
Southington, CT 06489-0246
Phone (203) 621-2079
Fax (203) 621-2989

This center presents workshops and seminars on aging and intergenerational programs. It publishes a newsletter, *Linkage,* for sharing resources and information.

Elvirita Lewis Foundation
Airport Park Plaza, Suite 144
255 N. El Cielo Road
Palm Springs, California 92262-6914

This foundation promotes understanding of aging through its aging awareness program. It also has some publications on intergenerational programs.

Generations Together
University of Pittsburgh
811 William Pitt Union
Pittsburgh, Pennsylvania 15260

Generations Together has pioneered numerous research programs and developed many model intergenerational programs. It also maintains a small reference/research library and publishes a newsletter, *Generations Together,* that contains the names and addresses of contact persons in almost every state.

Generations United
c/o Child Welfare League
440 First Street, N.W.
Suite 310
Washington, D.C. 20001

Generations United is a coalition of more than 100 national organizations concerned with intergenerational issues and programs. The coalition publishes a newsletter, *Newsline,* that contains information on programs and upcoming workshops and conferences.

National Association for the Education of Young Children (NAEYC)
1834 Connecticut Avenue, N.W.
Washington, D.C. 20009-5786

NAEYC publishes some materials on intergenerational programs. The organization sponsors workshops at its regional workshops and annual national conference.

Retired Senior Volunteer Program (RSVP)
517 N. Segoe Road
Suite 210
Madison, Wisconsin 53705-3108

RSVP promotes intergenerational programs through its chapters and advocates for intergenerational issues. It publishes a newsletter, *Intergenerational Clearinghouse Newsletter,* that shares information from programs throughout the country.

Terra Nova Films, Inc.
9848 S. Winchester Avenue
Chicago, Illinois 60643

Terra Nova Films releases many films dealing with intergenerational relationships and aging issues. A free catalogue is available, and films can be previewed for a minimal cost.

TABLES

Table 1:   Benefits of Intergenerational Programs for Children and Elders

FOR CHILDREN

Emotional and Social Benefits
Unconditional love/acceptance
Physical closeness/touching
Increased self-esteem
Additional adult attention
Another role outside the family

Tolerance and understanding
Positive relationship to male elders

Cognitive Benefits
Understanding of life cycle
Opportunity to learn skills of another
   generation
Stimulation of storytelling, reading,
   talking, playing

Sensory and Motor Benefits
Challenges to the senses
Awareness of need to exercise
across the lifespan

FOR ELDERS

Emotional and Social Benefits
Unconditional love/acceptance
Physical closeness/touching
Increased self-esteem
Relief from loneliness, boredom
Opportunity to help others and feel
   needed
Additional friendships
Topics for conversation
Sense of renewal, hope

Cognitive Benefits
Understanding of children today
Opportunity to share history

Stimulation of planning and
   interacting with children

Sensory and Motor Benefits
Challenges to the senses
Increased activity, both large and
   small muscle

Table 2:   Benefits and Concerns for Caregivers in Intergenerational Programs

BENEFITS   CONCERNS

For Early Childhood Staff   **For Early Childhood Staff**
Awareness of similarities across   Liability (off-site)
   lifespan, of needs, techniques
Sense of purpose, continuity   Physical
                                               arrangements/transportation
Innovative programming   Conflicting philosophy of staff
Education about aging   Financing
                                            Teachers' insecurity with elders

For Elder Care Staff   **For Elder Care Staff**
Awareness of similarities across   Liability (off-site)
   lifespan, of needs, techniques
Sense of purpose, continuity   Physical
                                               arrangements/transportation
Innovative programming   Conflicting philosophy of staff
Education about youth   Financing
                                            Staffs' insecurity with elders

Source: Adapted from "Intergenerational Activities Program," Broome County
Child Development Council, Inc., Binghamton, New York.

Table 3: A Sample Curriculum Web

PHYSICAL
Art Projects
Back Rubs
Bean Bag Toss
Bowling
Feely Bag
Hokey Pokey
Movement to Music
Painting
Parachute Ball
Rhythm Band
Sittercise
Walks

CULTURAL AWARENESS
Bring a Wheelchair to the Child-Care Center
Christmas
Clothing
Easter
Food
Games
Halloween
Hanukkah
Holidays
Kwanzaa
Martin Luther King Day
Mentally and Physically Challenged
Native American Day
President's Day
Share Other Languages
St. Patrick's Day
Thanksgiving
United Nation's Day
Valentine's Day

SOCIAL
Adopt a Grandparent
Animal Visits
Balloon Launch
Bingo/Board Games
Bubble Fun
Family Picture Collage
Friendship Chain/Quilt
Funny Hat Day
Get Well Cards
Hobbies
Holiday Gifts
Ice Cream Socials
Life Histories/Occupations
Lotto
Luncheons
Monthly Birthday Parties
Pen Pals
Pets
Picnics
Plays by the Children
Share and Tell
Sing-a-Longs
Storytelling
(Thumbbody Loves You)
Travelog
Visits from Children
Zoo Animals

LIFE CYCLES
A Long Time Ago
Babies/Wash Dolls
Bird Feeders
Bread Making
Family Pictures
Gardening
Hat Box
Pin Wheels
Planting Seeds
Seasons
Snowmen
Trees—Leaf Printing
Water Play
Weather

CONNECTIONS

INTERGENERATIONAL LINKS BETWEEN CHILDREN AND ELDERS

OUTINGS
Bird Watching
Dairy
Discovery World
Grocery Store
Library
Movies/Videos
Museums
Park
Watch Children/Courtyard
Zoo

COOKING
Ants on a Log
Applesauce
Bread
Butter
Decorate Cupcakes
Decorate Graham Crackers
Ice Cream
Lemonade Stand
Making Snacks
Milkshakes
Mulled Cider
Pancakes
Peanut Butter
Pear People
Pizza
Popcorn
Pretzels
Pumpkin Bread
Rainbow Sandwiches
Scrambled Eggs
Soup
Tasting Party
Tuna Boats

STORIES
Changes/Browne
Cycles, Cycles, Cycles/Ross
Emma/Kesselman
Grandma Is Somebody Special/Goldman
Grandpa/Borack
Love You Forever/Munch
Kevin's Grandma/Williams
Little Rabbit's Loose Tooth/Bate
My Visit to the Dinosaurs/Aliki
Now One Foot, Now the Other/de Paola
Strega Nona/de Paola
Tell me Grandma, Tell me Grandpa/Newman
The Quilt Story/Johnston
The Whale's Song/Sheldon
Watch Out for the Chicken Feet in Your Soup/de Paola
Wilfrid Gordon McDonald Partridge/Mem Fox

MANIPULATIVES
Clay
Crafts
Egg Dying and Decorating
Fruit and Vegetable Printing
Manicures/Hand Massages
Papier Mâché
Play Dough/Cookie Cutters
Puzzles
Sawdust Sculpture
Sewing Cards
Silly Putty
Sponge Painting
Watercolor
Woodworking

Source: Catherine Blount, McKinley Centre Intergenerational Program, Canton, Ohio.

Table 4: Elders' Favorite Kinds of Intergenerational Activities

TYPE OF ELDERS	BEST-LIKED CATEGORIES
Frail Elders	Short-term Gross motor Simple
Alzheimer's Elders	Gross motor Long-term
Community Elders	Cultural Process Generational Cognitive Rote Structured Passive

from the McKinley Centre Intergenerational Project